How to Create

ABUNDANCE

An Intender's Workbook

Zip-a-dee-do-da!

Published in 2019 by Anamcara Press LLC

Author © 2019 by Mitch Cearbhall, https://anamcara-press.com/our-newest-selections/mitch-cearbhall/

Photography © 2019 by Maureen Carroll
Book Cover Art by Jack Cleveland
Book design by Maureen Carroll
Palatino Linotype, Myriad Pro, Lithos Pro, and Jokeman.

Printed in the United States of America.
Imagination to Manifestation—How To Create Abundance is about intention and action. The hands-on workbook teaches methods to control your thinking and construct focused intentions to manifest the life you have only dreamed of having.

Excerpt of "All things are composed of Light..." from the website www.aquariuspapers.com, by Robert Wilkinson. Reprinted by permission of Robert Wilkinson. Excerpt of "Seven Virtures of a Warrior" from the website http://deer-tribe.com/, by Swiftdeer Reagan, Harley. Reprinted by permission of Mary Minor. Excerpt of "The Intenders of the Highest Good" from the website http://www.tonyburroughs.net/, by Tony Burroughs. Reprinted by permission of Tony Burroughs.

All rights reserved. No part of this publication may be reproduced, distributed, or transmitted in any form or by any means, including photocopying, recording, or other electronic or mechanical methods, without the prior written permission of the publisher, except in the case of brief quotations embodied in critical reviews and certain other noncommercial uses permitted by copyright law. For permission requests, write to the publisher, addressed "Attention: Permissions Coordinator," at this address:

ANAMCARA PRESS LLC
P.O. Box 442072, Lawrence, KS 66044
https://anamcara-press.com/

Ordering Information:
Quantity sales. Special discounts are available on quantity purchases. For details, contact the publisher at the address above.
Orders by U.S. trade bookstores and wholesalers. Please contact Ingram Distribution.

Publisher's Cataloging-in-Publication data
Cearbhall, Mitch., Author
Imagination to Manifestation: How to Create Abundance - An Intender's Workbook / Mitch Cearbhall

ISBN-13: Imagination to Manifestation, 978-1-941237-14-4 (paperback)
ISBN-13: Imagination to Manifestation, 978-1-941237-15-1 (ebook)
SELF-HELP/SELF-IMPROVEMENT; BODY, MIND, SPIRIT; PHILOSOPHY

Imagination to Manifestation

How to Create

ABUNDANCE

An Intender's Workbook

Mitch Cearbhall

Anamcara Press
Lawrence, KS

For Josh, Tim, MaKenna, Allie-Anne, Jaiden, Cheyanne, Kaitlyn, Christopher, Dylan, Sean, Hallie, and Jessica. Aim high and keep your aims in sight.

Contents

The Call of the Open Road..........................1

Follow a Higher Path................................17

Follow Your Intended Path......................27

The Path Of Imagination.........................39

The Rock In The Path...............................51

The Path With Heart.................................67

Our Common Path....................................79

The Path Of Transformation...................91

DEAR READER,

This little book is about intention and action. Research on consciousness demonstrates that manifesting your intentions—making your dreams come true—is rooted in your perception of the world. You were born able to create what you desire, and you remain able to create what you desire. My intention is to help you understand how the process works.

Today, there is a lot of information available about how we create and how our ability to create—to change ourselves and our world—is possible and ultimately relies on our beliefs. In the following eight chapters you'll be introduced to concepts that might intrigue you, or excite you, or confuse you, or that you might find stupid and ridiculous. Try to keep an open mind as you read, and consider this workbook a brief introduction to some new ways of thinking, or a reminder of some old.

In these pages, you'll learn methods to control your thinking. You'll learn how to construct focused intentions and follow through to manifest the reality you have only dreamed of having. You'll also learn how you can use your new skills to help others and change the world for the better.

Whether you're a beginner or a teacher, there are relevant exercises and activities to give you an opportunity to experience the change and not merely read about it, and to help others in their change process. At the end of the book you'll find a list of resources to help you continue your learning.

A free companion e-book of writing prompts is available on the publisher's website: anamcara-press.com.

Mitch Cearbhall

Heroic deeds were all conceiv'd in the open air.

Walt Whitman, "Song of the Open Road"

Chapter 1

THE CALL OF THE OPEN ROAD

A picture from a bygone era shows a young man, a child by today's standards, walking down a country road with a confident and contented smile upon his face. His clothes are worn and comfortable, and he carries just a few belongings tied to a stick that he balances on his shoulder, pointing skyward, as he skips along whistling and carefree.

The picture brings to mind simple joys: sunshine on shoulders with a hint of a cool breeze; a timeless, worry-free afternoon with no obligations; "hello-s" from neighbors, friends and strangers who have some free time to spend. No hurry, no worry, no fear, no tears. Just a welcoming walk down an inviting path—a path that leads to a bright future. Can you imagine being out on a country road, away from the traffic and hustle and bustle, away from the hum-drum of your everyday life? Out on the open road, you can see far and wide; you're not hedged in by buildings or obligations. You can spread wide your arms and breathe deeply the clean, fresh air.

Our world can feel hectic and heartless—a cold bone of a supper compared to the rich, succulent feast of a glorious past where the open road lay waiting, encouraging us to seek adventure.

How to Create Abundance

Where is the path of possibility now? How can we follow our dreams today? How do we find our way in this harsh, paved world?

Despite the pavement and the noise, the open road is still there for us to follow. Walt Whitman advised us to just start walking—to set off down the road and let your true path find you. He recommended venturing out into life, "afoot and lighthearted" in his poem, "Song of the Open Road." He believed "the long brown path" would lead us to where we intended to go. He also believed that we create our own "good fortune" along the way.

In his travels, Whitman gained insight into people and the forces of nature around him. He recognized while he wandered the countryside during the middle 19th century, that it is not easy to let go of the baggage we hold from the past. Instead, we carry it with us on our journeys. "Still here I carry my old delicious burdens," he lamented.

In spite of the heavy weight we may bear, he believed we should continue "forever alive, forever forward." Whitman recognized what physicists were just beginning to discover: life is energy.

Modern scientists have described this energy as being a vibration, like music is a vibration. String Theory says *everything* is made up of vibrating strings of pulsing energy, like a song. As you sing your life into being, you may not be aware of the melody you play. You may not recognize that you choose the tune and the tone. If you've been singing an unhappy or unsatisfactory song, you have the power to change the tune.

We've all heard "change your attitude!" It seems impossible to do in the moment. In order to change the tune, we need a change in our energy field. Refreshing sleep; long, heartfelt talks; physical activity; time spent in contemplation; good music; and even fuzzy kittens *do* change attitudes! We've all experienced this pleasant change from negative to positive

Call of the Open Road

energy and know it's possible. But how can we *deliberately* change our attitude and can we do it *at will*? This is the million-dollar question.

The Human Energy Field can be defined as the energy that surrounds and permeates our physical bodies. The ancient Chinese described this in terms of energy flow (Qi) through our chakras (energy centers) via the meridians (energy highways), and mapped how this energy moves through our bodies.

The Human Energy Field has been studied by Western science since the 1980s using the SQUID magnetometer (Superconducting Quantum Interference Device). SQUID is capable of detecting tiny biomagnetic fields associated with physiological activities in the body.

Sadly, there is as yet no machine to reset our energy field to base, or normal. Clearing the energy field requires, instead, a determined effort. It's not easy to change patterns—old habits and thoughts—that keep us where we are. As Whitman said, even when we step out onto the open road, we bring our "old delicious burdens" with us. Other people's "can'ts" and

> I CELEBRATE MYSELF,
> AND SING MYSELF,
> AND WHAT I ASSUME
> YOU SHALL ASSUME,
> FOR EVERY ATOM
> BELONGING TO ME AS
> GOOD BELONGS TO YOU.
>
> Walt Whitman

How to Create Abundance

"shouldn'ts" can create nagging doubts that disturb sleep and keep us from experiencing joy. These not-so-true messages from the past have to be put into context and rewritten in our own, current and more positive words.

STUCK IN BRAMBLES & THORNS

We may find ourselves stuck on a road we don't like. Fear, envy, resentment, and other negative emotions block our way forward. These negative emotions are caused by what we think. Our thoughts can spin and cycle downward off the path and into the ditch! We know when we think positive thoughts, we have positive emotions and feel good. And we know, conversely, if we think negative thoughts, we'll have negative emotions and feel bad. What we often *don't* know is how to take control of our thinking. In order to clear these negative emotions, we need to rethink things.

The most effective way to begin to rethink things is to practice forgiveness. Forgive yourself and others in order to clear your energy field. Forgive yourself and others in order to take control of your thinking and get on the right path—the path that's right for you today.

> ONCE YOU REPLACE NEGATIVE THOUGHTS WITH POSITIVE ONES, YOU'LL START HAVING POSITIVE RESULTS.
> — Willie Nelson

When we forgive, we are able to move forward. If you can't forgive yourself and others, you remain stuck in the past. To step onto the path of forgiveness is to take a step forward out onto the open road—to step toward a path of joy and a powerful future, a future where you are empowered. Research shows that forgiving yourself may be the best way to begin to live the life of your choice rather than a life of someone else's choosing or of chance.

The first step on this path of forgiveness is to acknowledge that no one is perfect. No one can do it all, have it all, or be it all. We each have our own unique talents. We each have our flaws. Forgiving sounds so easy, and yet it is one of the most difficult tasks we need to do.

We all carry those "delicious burdens" Whitman talked about—baggage from the past that can hover like ghosts in the shadows. A parent, or other adult, may have told you that you "could not" or "should not," or said you were "bad" or "stupid." Or you may have feelings of inferiority from watching others receive praise or rewards when you did not. Often, we don't remember where the messages came from. Sometimes we don't even know what the messages are; we just have a vague sense of doom when we venture forward.

Practice forgiving yourself for your real or perceived shortcomings. It will make it easier to forgive others for their transgressions against you. And you will be able to move forward with positive thoughts that will enable you to achieve the life of your dreams.

HOW TO FORGIVE

Stanford University completed a study that determined the benefits of forgiveness. Reported in *the Journal Of Clinical Psychology*, it was the first large, randomized study (259 adults) that experimented with forgiveness intervention.

The study compared the effects of forgiveness intervention training using a control group who received no intervention. The participants who were given training on forgiveness techniques completed six 90-minute sessions that included training in *cognitive disputation, mindfulness meditation,* and *guided imagery.* The study showed how important forgiveness is to our perception of well-being.

How to Create Abundance

Cognitive Disputation

Dr. Frederick Luskin provided cognitive disputation therapy to the intervention group by asking them questions. Cognitive disputation is a process of questioning that challenges your views and perceptions of yourself and the world. This questioning of your internal rules may help you to perceive things differently.

Guided Imagery

Guided imagery is a process of vividly imagining a place or experience in order to bring about relaxation, improve performance, and improve health. It is a simple process you can achieve in a few steps with a little practice.

Research shows if you need to have surgery, it will benefit you to use guided imagery, especially if your surgeon also uses guided imagery. *The American Journal of Obstetrics and Gynecology* reported a study (one of many) that tested how mental imagery compared to hands-on practice when learning basic surgical procedures.

The study tested 65 medical students divided into three random groups: Group A received three sessions of physical practice suturing a pigs foot; Group B received two sessions of physical practice and one of imagery; and Group C received one session of physical practice and two of imagery. The results of the study showed that physical practice, followed by mental imagery rehearsal, was statistically equal to additional physical practice. Wow! Just imagine!

> A MAN IS BUT THE PRODUCT OF HIS THOUGHTS. WHAT HE THINKS, HE BECOMES.
>
> Mahatma Gandhi

Mindfulness Meditation

Mindfulness meditation is a technique that teaches how to be "mindful." What does that mean? My personal definition is: fully aware of your body, thinking, and emotions while being at ease and relaxed, and non-judgemental. In this attentive, non-agitated state perception widens. You can step away from your emotions about a person or situation, and consider your response dispassionately.

Like other meditation techniques, it takes practice to achieve mindfulness; and like Cognitive Disputation, it might be best to seek an expert's assistance, but these techniques are things you can learn about and practice on your own.

Study participants, who learned through *cognitive disputation, mindfulness meditation,* and *guided imagery* to take less personal offense and blame others less frequently, showed a 70% drop in the degree of hurt they felt as compared to what they reported at the beginning of the study. Anger decreased significantly in the trained group, and optimism increased.

EXERCISE I
Guided Imagery

Find a comfortable, quiet place and relax. Make sure you have 10-20 minutes of uninterrupted time.

Close your eyes and imagine your favorite place in nature; it could be a sunny beach, a beautiful mountain meadow, or your tree house when you were a child—anywhere you feel relaxed and at ease.

Imagine yourself enjoying this wonderful place. Picture every detail, including what you're doing and how you feel.

Return to your quiet place for a few minutes each day and continue to visualize more detail each time.

How to Create Abundance

WRITING for SELF DETERMINATION
ASSIGNMENT I (a) Forgiveness

Spend no more than 20 minutes writing on one of the topics listed below. Repeat the exercise on a different day in the same week for a total of four writing sessions of no more than 20 minutes each. Then stop. Don't write on this topic further.

Research shows this kind of journaling can help us think through a problem or issue. Spending longer on the topic may increase negativity and contribute to ruminating.

1. I forgive myself for...
2. I forgive my parent/guardian for...
3. I forgive my sibling/friend for...

Notably, physical symptoms of stress decreased in the trained group. Overall, the study showed that self-forgiveness and forgiving others can improve health and wellness, and make people feel better.

FORGETNESS

It's not so easy to say, "I forgive you." It is harder still to feel and act upon forgiveness. The process of forgiveness requires two actions: forgiveness and *forgetness*. Forgiveness is best achieved through understanding—you find a way to understand another's actions or words. Why did they break your trust? If you can put yourself in their shoes, you may be able to understand them. Understanding them makes it much easier to forgive them. Might you have done the same thing if you were in their circumstances? Even if the answer is "no," even if you cannot find understanding, perhaps you can suspend your judgment in order to forgive another. Practicing the techniques listed above can help.

Judging others and holding grudges go hand-in-hand. Holding a grudge requires you to feed your envy or resentment. Like anything else, it needs the fuel of your thoughts to grow. If you focus your thoughts on forgiveness, in time you'll find it.

Forgetness is much more difficult to achieve than forgiveness. Forgetness is different than forgetfulness in that you don't actually lose your memory of the issue or incident. And that is good. There is a reason we have a memory—so that we don't keep putting ourselves in uncomfortable or dangerous situations. People find healing when they are able to forgive someone who abused them, but forgiving an abuser can only happen after the abuse stops. Forgiving doesn't mean condoning or accepting abuse.

Forgetness is the process by which you end ruminating over the issue, you stop bringing it up, and you are able to move beyond it. The memory is still there, but you are not dwelling on that memory. (This is not an easy process for anyone, and there may be physical/mental conditions that make it even more difficult for some people.)

RUMINATING

Ruminating is what farmers call it when a cow chews her cud (food) over and over again in order to digest it properly. Ruminating is also what we call it when you get a thought stuck in your head (particularly and usually a negative thought) that just won't go away. The thought persists morning, noon, and night. You wake up thinking this negative thought or considering this negative situation, replaying the incident in your head instead of thinking other, more important, more healthy things. When your friends ask you how you're doing, it is the first thing you think of and want to talk

How to Create Abundance

about. When you try to stop thinking of the problem person or issue, the negative thinking becomes even stronger, dispelling other, nicer thoughts. You might feel as though you can't control your thinking at all!

How do you stop it? *Can* you control the thoughts in your head? Thankfully, the answer is "yes." You are capable of selecting what you think about. Two things are necessary in order for you to control your thinking. First, you must be aware that you have *a choice*; and second, you must consciously make the choice.

Imagine thought as like the Milky Way galaxy. Instead of thousands of stars floating around, there are thousands of thoughts floating around. They are all there, any and every thought you might conceive of thinking—good, bad, and in between. You are able to select from this cosmic stream anything that you desire. You can ignore the negative bits while still being aware that they exist. You don't have to select them for review. You may instead mull over the joyful, the pleasant, the peaceful, the exciting. Turn away from what you don't want; choose actively what you *do* want to think about.

Mark Waldman, author of *10 Mind Blowing Discoveries About the Human Brain*, reports that human beings cannot focus on a positive and negative experience or memory at the same time. It is just not possible to dwell on something you enjoy *and* something you dislike at the same time. Go ahead, try it!

"So if you're feeling pain, do something pleasurable and the sensation of pain will decrease. Since consciousness is limited, you have a choice: you can ruminate on negativity or focus on solution-based goals, but you can't do both at the same time," Waldman asserts.

STINKIN' THINKIN'

Sometimes the negative stories we tell ourselves take on a life of their own. We might see things as black & white, all or nothing, even when others point out the grays. Or we might over generalize—engage in always/never thinking, or jump to conclusions before we have needed information. Dr. David Burns calls this kind of negativity "Stinkin' Thinkin'" (ST) and identifies 10 forms of twisting thinking that take us around in circles.

"ST language fosters a bad way of thinking that makes you believe you will fail, that bad things will happen to you, or that you are not a very good person," according to *Cambridge Advanced Learner's Dictionary & Thesaurus*.

Stinkin' Thinkin' is perfectly normal. According to Burns, everybody engages in it at sometime. "Where we mess up in our lives is when we let these conversations take on a life of their own." Burns reminds us that these thoughts are "irrational, because they have little or no basis in reality," but that doesn't make them any easier to prevent.

> We cannot prevent birds from flying over our heads, but we can keep them from making nests on top of our heads. Similarly, bad thoughts sometimes appear in our minds, but we can choose whether or not we allow them to live there and create a nest for themselves.
>
> ~ Leo Tolstoy

How to Create Abundance

We can learn to identify these types of negative, circular thinking and counter them. Burns recommends keeping a journal. "As you learn to better identify them, you can then learn how to start answering them back with rational arguments. In this manner, you can work to turn your internal conversation back to being a positive in your life, instead of a running negative commentary." *(See list of the 12 types of Stinkin' Thinkin' in Appendix A.)*

TECHNIQUES FOR CONTROLLING YOUR THOUGHTS

Below are seven techniques for controlling ruminating, negative thinking. Explore them, ask others how they control their negative thoughts, and experiment until you find a technique that allows you to acknowledge the negative thought and then successfully move on to something else. Give yourself time. Habits are hard to change.

1. If there is a word, sentence, or picture stuck in your mind that you just can't shake, say "stop!"
2. Replace the negative thought with another more positive, or neutral thought, sentence, or picture.
3. Pay attention to your feelings when you're thinking negative thoughts. Recognize that your thinking produced the emotion, and not the other way around. Where did that thought come from? Can you change or alter it using the techniques above?
4. Pay attention to what you are feeding your mind; stop watching and listening to things that upset you that are avoidable. Why watch news after work when you're stressed, or a slasher movie when you're depressed?
5. Pay attention to what you're feeding your body.

Call of the Open Road

Do you notice any mood changes 1-24 hours after eating certain foods? Research shows that what we eat has an impact on how we feel. For example, some food allergies can make people feel groggy or agitated. When we feel physically bad, we are more likely to think negatively and engage in ruminating.

6. Reward yourself for stopping negative thoughts when they pop up. You deserve it!

7. Savor positive moments. Our human brain tends to emphasize negative experiences over positive experiences. So the next time something positive happens, and it will, make a big deal out of it; put it firmly in your memory.

We can free ourselves from the past desires of other people (who may no longer even be in our lives) by forgiving and forgetting. And we can identify the kinds of stinkin' thinkin' we engage in and learn to prevent the vicious circle of thoughts—or the circle of vicious thoughts. We can then move forward on our own path, the path we truly desire to walk. That is, if we can figure out what we want!

INTENTIONS EXPERIMENT I

Intender's Journal

Create an Intender's Journal or notebook. Spend 5 minutes each day, starting today, writing in your Intenders Journal. Write down those things that you intend to do, think, or say. Pay attention to your language. Review weekly for successes.

How to Create Abundance

WRITING for SELF DETERMINATION
ASSIGNMENT I (b) Positive Swap

Make a list of **three negative statements** that you think or say. For example, "I'm a terrible cook," or "I'm a klutz," or "they don't like me."

Next, make a list of three replacement statements that you can memorize and substitute for the negative statement. For example, "I'm a creative cook," "I'm graceful" or "I am loved." If this feels strange to you, select the lyrics of a song you enjoy, or a line from a poem.

The goal is to identify the negative thinking and substitute something positive in its place. I've used the Buddhist chant *Soka Gakkai* (Nam-myoho-rengi-kyo) successfully. (*See information about this chant in Appendix II.*)

Warning: positive thinking ought not replace cautious or critical thinking. If something is bothering you, there might be a good reason. Examine the reality of the negative thinking. "What's the worst that could happen?" Sometimes it's necessary to take action, rather than chant. You can still think positively about the outcome of the situation or circumstance.

- _____
- _____
- _____
- _____
- _____
- _____
- _____
- _____
- _____

As a single footstep will not make a path on the earth,
so a single thought will not make a pathway in the mind.
To make a deep physical path, we walk again and again.
To make a deep mental path, we must think over and over
the kind of thoughts we wish to dominate our lives.

~ Henry David Thoreau

Every journey begins with the first step of articulating the intention, and then becoming the intention.

Bryant McGil, "Voice of Reason"

Chapter 2

FOLLOW A HIGHER PATH

People frequently want things that aren't good for them. It is easy to confuse pleasure with happiness, and too much pleasure seems to lead to unhappiness. In order to realize your dreams, and be happy with the outcome, set your intentions on the highest good.

What is "the highest good?" Perhaps the best definition is: *intending for the betterment of all*.

Some people insist that there is no such thing as "highest good." They argue that from our limited human perspective we can't see the outcome of our intentions, and so we might just as well intend for our own betterment. While it is true that we don't always know what we want, or see what truly is in our best interest, it is likely that what is *truly* in our best interest *is* for the highest good.

For example, let's say I intend to live in an extra large house in the country. Even though it's just my spouse and me, I like the idea of having a lot of room for entertaining and I like having beautiful scenery around me. An ecologist might inform me that my choice is not for the highest good because of the negative impact of heating and cooling the large house, displacing wildlife, and commuting. If I really think about it (or experience it for a few months or years) I might come to the conclusion that caring for a big house and property takes

How to Create Abundance

a lot of time. I miss being close to my friends and activities, and the commute is stressful. Perhaps I'd really be happier in a roomy loft downtown.

Sometimes we have to look behind our stated or superficial intention and look within. If the intention is not for the highest good, then we are not likely to achieve it or enjoy it much if we do. It is worthwhile to spend some time in self-reflection before setting intentions in order to attain that which will create happiness.

NEEDS, WANTS, DESIRES, INTENTIONS

When setting intentions it is good to know what you want. As illustrated above, we might think we know what we want and discover later that we didn't want it after all. A way to avoid this mistake is to understand the difference between *needs, wants, desires, and intentions.*

Needs: A need is something that if you don't have it, you will suffer long term pain. Having your needs met requires help from outside of yourself. People need what is basic to life: food, water, shelter, a sense of belonging, and love.

Wants: A want is something that if you don't have it, you usually suffer short term pain. Having your wants met does not always require outside assistance. Our wants are often fleeting and changeable, but specific. People often want things we think we lack: a particular kind of food, drink, home, or attention.

Desires: A desire is something that if you don't have it, you're perfectly happy without it, there is no pain. Desires may be more broad and less specific or limited

> WITHIN YOU
> IS THE
> DIVINE CAPACITY
> TO MANIFEST
> & ATTRACT
> ALL YOU DESIRE.
>
> Wayne Dyer

A Higher Path

than wants. People often desire achievements such as: recognition, praise, and emotional security rather than desiring material things. Desires may seem to be just out of reach.

Intentions: An intention is mindfully created—it involves making a decision. To achieve our intentions requires intellectual desire, emotional belief, and physical action. You can *desire* and take no action. An intention motivates you to action. Taking action can lead to accomplishment

The key to a joyous, fulfilled life is to make your needs into wants (you don't *have* to have it), your wants into desires (you're perfectly happy without it), and your desires into intentions (you mindfully determine what you are going to have, do, or be).

WHAT DO YOU DESIRE?

Sometimes we get stuck in a place where we can't see our own desires. This can happen when we follow messages

EXERCISE II
GIVE TO YOURSELF

Try this experiment: massage your left palm with your right thumb for 15 seconds then switch and rub your right palm with your left thumb for 15 seconds. Finally, run your fingers lightly over your arms slowly for a few seconds. What are your thoughts? How do you feel?

This quick, pleasant technique decreases negative thoughts and emotions because physical pleasure releases dopamine, a neurotransmitter that can make you feel good. I use it when I travel on airplanes to help enjoy the flight and reduce stress.

How to Create Abundance

from others, or messages that aren't true for us anymore. We can lose sight of our desires when we are busy taking care of other people, or we can find ourselves overwhelmed by the busy-ness of everyday life. We might hardly notice that our desires have been tossed by the wayside.

In order to better know what *you* desire *today*, consider these three questions:

1. Where will you be and what will you be doing in five years? (It doesn't matter where you'll actually be in five years, answering this question gives you ideas to pursue.)
2. What are your values and how can you be true to them?
3. What are you curious about—what makes you passionate?

When we don't know what we desire, it may mean that we are stuck in fear or apathy. Or we think that our desires are out of reach. Take some action even if you don't know what you want. Let that action be giving. *Give to others if you don't know what you want to receive for yourself.* This action can lead you to your true desires.

Life without intention is like an ocean with a rock-cliff shore, and you are in deep water. If you take no action you're likely to get bashed against the rocks by the first big wave. Carl Jung said, "that which we do not bring to consciousness appears in our lives as fate." When we aren't conscious of our real desires—when we don't know what we want—then our lives are in the hands of the roaring waves and we might get bashed against the rocks. Instead swim! Even if you swim in the wrong direction, at least you are moving and learning, you can always change directions.

A Higher Path

GAIN FROM GIVING

When you spend time caring or doing for another you will benefit. How does this work? Aren't caregivers stressed-out? The New York Times reported that "while caregivers were indeed more stressed, they still had lower mortality rates than non-caregivers over eight years of follow-up." According to Dr. Lisa Fredman, a Boston University epidemiologist. They also maintained "stronger physical performance than non-caregivers," and "caregivers did significantly better on memory tests." Wow! If you want to stay healthy, alert, and alive, then give!

Author Stephen Post, *Why Good Things Happen to Good People*, wrote that people with chronic illness, like HIV & Multiple Sclerosis, benefited noticeably from giving to others. Another study led by Doug Oman at UC Berkeley demonstrated over a 5 year period that older people who volunteered were more likely to continue to be alive and well than non-volunteers. Why? Helping others feels good and it gives life purpose.

Why not intend to possess millions of dollars? You might be thinking, "I can really help people if I just had a lot of money." Maybe you could. Money can also be a burden and a responsibility. Money may make the world go 'round, but it does not make people happy. Many research studies have demonstrated that possessing money in excess of our

> THE MOST DIFFICULT THING IS THE DECISION TO ACT, THE REST IS MERELY TENACITY. THE FEARS ARE PAPER TIGERS. YOU CAN DO ANYTHING YOU DECIDE TO DO. YOU CAN ACT TO CHANGE AND CONTROL YOUR LIFE, AND THE PROCEDURE, THE PROCESS IS ITS OWN REWARD.
> *Amelia Earhart*

needs does not increase our perception of joy and happiness in our lives. "Money can't buy me love," sang the Beatles.

"People who are highly focused on materialistic values have lower personal well-being and psychological health than those who believe that materialistic pursuits are relatively unimportant," according to Tim Kassar in *The High Price of Materialism*.

In a study of 792 well-off adults, more than half reported that wealth didn't bring them more happiness, and a third of those with assets greater than $10 million, said that money brought more problems than it solved. Although those with higher incomes report being somewhat more satisfied with their lives, studies of how they actually spend their days find that they don't spend time in any more enjoyable activities than their poorer friends. In fact, they are more likely to experience daily anxiety and anger, Sonja Lyubomirsky points out in *The How of Happiness: A Scientific Approach to getting the life you want*.

Does it sound fun to sit alone and count money? Probably not. What would you do or buy with the money? Set your intention on that which you truly desire, not on a pile of dirty coins or bills. Instead of concentrating on money, think about what you'd do with it.

PLEASURE OR HAPPINESS?

Lyubomirsky sums up the current research on happiness: "50 percent of individual differences in happiness are governed by genes, 10 percent by life circumstance, and the remaining 40 percent by what we do and how we think — that is, our intentional activities and strategies... If we observe genuinely happy people, we shall find that they do not just sit around being contented. They make things happen."

When people achieve their passing or petty wants, it doesn't bring them lasting happiness, instead they only want more. This is because happiness is the outcome of a deeper process. According to author and happiness researcher Mark

A Higher Path

Manson (*On Happiness,* http://markmanson.net/), "It's not the end results that define our ideal selves. It's not finishing the marathon that makes us happy; it's achieving a difficult, long-term goal that does."

People appear to have a baseline level of happiness, and momentary pleasure just gives a little boost, not a lasting impact. This is why seeking momentary pleasure doesn't create lasting happiness. We can increase our baseline happiness over time. And that, says Manson, "is the ticket to happiness—not a new car, not a fancier job, not a more attractive partner—but a permanent shift in the baseline happiness you continually return to despite whatever external factors occur in your life."

A major way to inch your baseline happiness upwards is to gain control. Research shows that people who report being the happiest believe they have control over their lives. As Manson points out, "You can be rich, famous, have everything you ever wanted, but if you feel like you had no control of it, like you didn't deserve it or earn it, you will be miserable."

So to be happy, set your intentions on the highest good—choose what direction to swim or walk, roll, etc., and adjust your course as needed. When you find obstacles in your path, keep your vision and steer around them. You are powerful and in control of your destiny.

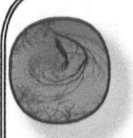

INTENTIONS EXPERIMENT II
Intending for the Highest Good

Write down an intention that involves giving. It could be giving time, energy, or smiles as well as things or money. Write what you want to give without using the words "if" or "but." Take your time; make sure your words really reflect your intention.

How to Create Abundance

WRITING for SELF DETERMINATION
ASSIGNMENT II Receiving

Can you remember a time when you were given something that you didn't ask for, something that you really wanted or needed? It could have been a helping hand, a friendly word, or just a smile. How did it make you feel? Did the gift freely given to you encourage you to give to others? Spend a few minutes writing down your thoughts.

- _____
- _____
- _____
- _____
- _____
- _____
- _____
- _____
- _____
- _____
- _____
- _____
- _____
- _____
- _____
- _____
- _____
- _____

FATE OR DESTINY

Fate is the path that is predetermined by our lack of attention to our choices. Destiny is the open-ended patterns of possibilities and probabilities that are fashioned and directed through conscious choices and freewill.

If one is unconscious about having choices, then they accept the experiences that they allow others to dictate for them. The result is a fate of other-determined expectations that exclude personal vision.

~Jamie Sams

*Dare to dream!
If you did not have the capability to make your wildest wishes come true, your mind would not have the capacity to conjure such ideas in the first place...*
Anthon St. Maarten,
"Divine Living"

Chapter 3

FOLLOW YOUR INTENDED PATH

What are intentions and how are they different from wishes or hopes? The following definitions are from the Oxford English Dictionary:

Wish: "Expressing a desire that the event may happen or that the fact may prove to be so, and often implying some want of confidence or fear of the opposite." Synonyms include "crave," "long," and "yearn." A typical use is "I wish I could…"

Hope: "Expectation of something desired; desire combined with expectation." Hope is ideally coupled with belief. A typical use is: "We can only hope…"

Intend: An intention is a "Strenuous exertion of the mind or will; earnest attention, intentness; resolution, determination." To intend is to "direct one's thoughts or faculties" or "to apply oneself to do something." Synonyms include "purpose" "endeavor" and "assert." A typical use might be "What do you intend to do?"

As you can tell, these words have very different meanings. "If wishes were horses, beggars would ride," is an old English saying that means: it's useless to wish, you'll achieve better results with action. And it is true! Wishing and hoping with

How to Create Abundance

no action and follow through leaves us feeling wistful, full of: "vague, regretful longing."

Setting an intention is determining something. We usually follow through on things we determine to do. We usually don't follow through on our vague wishes.

YES & NO

Is there someone (or are you) telling you that you can't achieve your dream? Are you thinking "no" instead of "yes"?

NO! is a powerful word. Hearing and saying, or even just thinking the word "no" creates stress and tension in most people. Andrew Newberg M.D. and Mark Robert Waldman have done research on the impact of hearing and saying the word "no." People who saw the word "no" flashed for just one second experienced a rush of stress-producing chemicals—just one second!

Saying "no," instead of only seeing it, had an even stronger impact on study participants. And ruminating released even more "destructive chemicals," according to *Psychology Today* magazine, August 2012.

Worst of all, negative thinking has a snowball effect, leading to other negative thoughts. And if you spend time with negative people engaging in negative conversation, you'll both feel worse.

> **Our physical response to negative thoughts:**
> our heart beats faster, blood pressure goes up, our hands get colder, we breathe faster, our muscles tighten, our hands may sweat.
>
> **Our physical response to positive thoughts:**
> heart rate slows, blood pressure lowers, hands get warmer, breathing slows, muscles relax.

"Yes" solves problems; "no" closes minds. "Yes" provides an opening or beginning for something further to happen;

"no" ends further discovery or interaction. "Yes" makes people smile; "no" is usually accompanied with a frown.

Unfortunately, "yes" does not provoke our brain to a sudden release of chemicals that make us feel good in the same intense way that "no" creates a sudden release of stress-producing chemicals that make us feel bad. This means we have to work harder at the positive thoughts.

THE LAW OF ATTRACTION

The law of attraction is a well known concept that means like attracts like. When we clear our minds of negative thoughts, and forgive ourselves and others, we create space; space that can now be filled with positive thoughts, attractive thoughts—thoughts that attract what we want!

The Law of Atraction has been a hot topic for a long time. From Greek philosophers who searched for the meaning of life to modern film goers looking for *The Secret*, people have quested for the ability to make their dreams come true.

The authors of *The Secret*, a 2006 film and book, assert that by believing in a desired outcome, people can attract what they intend. In general, the Law of Attraction asserts that if we expect something negative to happen, it will. If we expect something positive to happen, it will.

> REALIZE THAT NOW, IN THIS MOMENT OF TIME, YOU ARE CREATING. YOU ARE CREATING YOUR NEXT MOMENT. THAT IS WHAT'S REAL.
>
> Sara Paddison

How to Create Abundance

Through our thinking we create our lives, according to the Law of Attraction. But I prefer the word "mold" to "create" when talking about the level of control our intentions can exert over our existence. It is different to mold a lump of clay than to create it. We have to deal with the lump of clay we're given, but we have a lot of control in how we mold that clay.

Current research in neuroscience shows that our ability to "mold our clay" through intention is a real, biological phenomena that can be seen and measured. Science is discovering the way we think about and voice our intentions has a direct effect on their outcome. Are we wishing or intending? Are we saying "yes" or saying "no"?

WORDS THAT WORK

Do your words reflect what you really desire, or are they focused on what you don't want? There are three important guidelines for putting your intentions into words that work:

1. Be Aware Of Your Motivations
2. Change Your Language
3. Be Determined

1. *Be Aware Of Your Motivations*

Are your intentions for the highest good? Sometimes we have to look behind our stated or superficial intention and look within our hearts. I might say, and even believe, that I'm doing this project for the highest good, when really I mostly crave recognition. My desire for recognition does not negate my desire to help other people. By acknowledging my motives, I may prevent self-deception. Try not to fool yourself! Rationalization is a steep hill. You can climb up too high and find you're unable to get back down again without falling.

It is worthwhile to spend some time in self-reflection before setting your intentions in order to manifest the dreams you want to share with others.

2. Change Your Language

What are you saying? Do your words reflect what you really want, or are they focused on what you don't want? When we focus on what we don't want, then that is where we put our energy—on what we don't want. One frustrated intender explained that she had intended consciously for more money. Days later she was offered overtime at work. Working more was not her intention. But the universe is like a mirror—your intentions are likely to manifest quite literally. Be careful what you ask for, and *how* you ask for it!

How we use language impacts our perception. We build and carry our thoughts with words. It's more difficult to see this if you know only one language. When you learn a second language, you see that some thoughts can be communicated easily in some languages, and with much more difficulty, if at all, in other languages. For example, the Danish word "Hygge" doesn't have an English equivalent. We have to use whole sentences to describe one Scandinavian word!

Alice laughed: "There's no use trying," she said; "one can't believe impossible things."

"I daresay you haven't had much practice," said the Queen. "When I was younger, I always did it for half an hour a day. Why, sometimes I've believed as many as six impossible things before breakfast."

~ Lewis Carroll

How to Create Abundance

HYGGE: "A quality of cosiness and comfortable conviviality that engenders a feeling of contentment or well-being (regarded as a defining characteristic of Danish culture.) As in: 'why not follow the Danish example and bring more hygge into your daily life?' And as modifier: 'count on candlelight—almost a requirement for that special hygge experience."—From the Oxford Online Dictionary.

Put your intentions into words that work by using language that is *positive*, *present*, and *specific*. As you change your language, notice how your intent may shift, sometimes in eye-opening ways. By making specific changes in the language you use, being aware of your motivation for setting the intention, and staying focused and determined, you can achieve your dreams.

Use *positive*, *present*, and *specific* language:

Be Positive: Use positive construction. Don't use, "I'm never going to eat sweets again." Instead use, "I am a healthy eater." Or instead of, "I intend to have no debt," try, "I am financially comfortable." Experiment until you find language that focuses on the positive achievement.

Be Present: Make your intentions present tense—not if, when; not then, now. "I am healthy and fit," as opposed to, "I will be healthy and fit." You are convincing yourself as you intend. The next step is to believe yourself!

Be Specific: Is your intention too broad? "I intend love and happiness for all," is a great intention, if unmeasurable. More specific intentions may give you more measurable results. For example, "I intend to give and receive love every day."

Your Intended Path

3. Be Determined

No more wishin' and hopin'. It is time for intending—determine what you are going to do and do it. Don't become fixated or ruminate about your intention. Instead, as with any other decision, take action. If you intend to eat sushi for dinner, you don't stand around wishing you had sushi—you make it, order it, or go get it!

An intention is like an arrow. You get your target in site, you aim with precision, you follow through keeping your eye on the target, then you shoot the arrow toward the goal. If your site (sight) has been true, then sooner or later... bam! Your intention is achieved.

Determine with the Spirit

Most people determine with their minds in our modern society. We typically believe that we *should* make our deci-

---

INTENTIONS EXPERIMENT III

Constructing Intentions

Construct three intentions using only positive, present, and specific language. Begin with the words, "I intend..." Don't use "wish" or "hope."

Positive: For example, instead of saying, "I intend to never miss my child's recital again," say, "I intend to regularly attend my child's recitals."

Present: Rather than, "I will begin to exercise," try, "I am fit and limber, and enjoy my daily exercise routine."

Specific: "I intend to make more money from my job." Instead of a raise, you might get overtime! Instead try, "I intend to earn a higher wage from my job, and have plenty of leisure time."

(See list of the 12 example intentions in Appendix B.)

How to Create Abundance

sions with our thinking minds. However, making a purely intellectual decision may not be for the best. We may not have thought things through, our thinking might not be broad or inclusive enough, or our thinking may be clouded by emotions, for example, doubt.

If you ponder upon it, it makes more sense to receive inspiration with the mind, to keep a mind receptive to ideas—an open mind—and it's best to make our decisions from a less intellectual and more spiritual perspective.

According to Kenneth Meadows in his writing about Native American beliefs, many traditional Native Americans think people should determine with their spirits, and receive with their minds. Western thinking has mixed this order up, Meadows asserts, and this has led to pain and suffering.

Problems happen when we decide with our minds, according to Meadows:

> "Principles and ethics are expressions of the spirit which has to do with the INTENT and WILL. Rules and laws are activities of the mind. Laws are fashioned in the mind in an effort to establish and safeguard principles and ethics, that is, to express the thought behind everything that is. When we obey a law in accordance with its intent we are carrying out the spirit of that law (determining with the Spirit.) We may, however, carry out the letter of the law, that is by mental application follow it literally, yet act contrary to its spirit and intent (determining with the mind.)"

Traditional Native American belief also encourages us to give with our emotions and hold with our body. We may instead give with ourselves physically, but hold our emotions tight. Meadows warns of the consequences of these interchanges:

> "By holding onto our emotions we are locking up our heart. We are often afraid to let our emotions express how we really feel because we think that by so doing we are making ourselves vulnerable. We think it

best to express our feelings through physical things and modern society is fully geared up to help us to do this. Love feelings and emotions are expressed through the provision of physical objects—television; videos...Even love can often become a purely physical athletic act measured on performance. Yet the most valid expression of love is the giving of oneself and the desire for the happiness of the loved one, without strings or conditions. True love is unconditional. Instead we give with the body and offer a sexual love that is only a physical expression. We hold on to what should have been given—our emotions—which is our love energy in motion."

Love is the most powerful energy we possess. Set your intentions from a place of love—for the highest good—and you'll set your love energy into motion. Remain positive, pres-

EXERCISE III
DETERMINE WITH THE SPIRIT
From Kenneth Meadows, Earth Medicine

Our energy system was designed to be espressed:

DETERMINE with the SPIRIT
RECEIVE with the MIND
GIVE with the EMOTIONS
HOLD with the BODY

But many of us were raised to:

DETERMINE with the MIND
RECEIVE with the SPIRIT
GIVE with the BODY
HOLD with the EMOTIONS

How might you experience your life differently if you shifted your perspective?

How to Create Abundance

ent, specific, and determined and you will see your dreams come into view at just the right time.

When you learn to attend to your language—what you think and say—it is like adjusting your course on a sail boat. It might seem like a slight adjustment, but it is a big ocean and slight adjustments can lead to big changes in direction over time.

WRITING for SELF DETERMINATION ASSIGNMENT III Words

Take some time to consider "what is my deepest personal value." Write down words. Then try switching the emphasis from deepest to *"personal"* value. Write down all of the words you imagine.

- Which of the words resonates most with you?
- Which one feels good?

Meditate on that **one** word; it might just be your best tool for finding calm in difficult situations according to researchers Andrew Newberg M.D. and Mark Robert Waldman.

- _____
- _____
- _____
- _____
- _____
- _____
- _____
- _____
- _____
- _____

If you hear a voice within you say "You cannot paint," then by all means paint, and that voice will be silenced.
~Van Gogh

What happens is of little significance compared with the stories we tell ourselves about what happens. Events matter little, only stories of events affect us.

Rabih Alameddine, "The Hakawati"

Chapter 4

THE PATH OF IMAGINATION

Whether you wish upon a star, make a vow, or shake your fist and curse, what you *believe* matters. You mold your reality with your beliefs. When you can imagine something is possible, you can create that possibility. If you cannot believe it, then it's not real for you.

Our beliefs about the past determine how we remember our past, and our beliefs about the future determine what our future becomes. We believe the stories we tell ourselves, even when they are not factual.

Our memories change. Research in neuroscience has shown that each time we remember something, the memory of it is slightly different from previous memories—it is not like there is a movie being replayed in our brains. Instead, our memories are doing something more like re-painting a picture. Each replica is going to be a bit different.

George Musser, writer for Science Magazine, describes how this works: "We store only bits and pieces of what happened—a smattering of impressions we weave together into what feels like a seamless narrative. When we retrieve a memory, we also rewrite it, so that the time next we go to remember it, we don't retrieve the original memory but the last one we recollected. So, each time we tell a story, we embellish it, while remaining genuinely convinced of the veracity of our memories."

How to Create Abundance

In addition to creating memories of events that may never have happened, conversely we might have no recollection of events that actually occurred.

Neuroscience research has not determined just where and how memory is stored, but researchers are sure that our perception of reality is very selective, even distorted. Although we are biologically wired for intention, in order to be an effective intender, we first need to understand how our distorted perception impacts our view of the world. Effective intending requires accurate perception.

OUR TWISTED PERCEPTION

Our selective, sometimes twisted perception has been measured in many research studies on "Inattentional Blindness"—a bizarre inability to see something obvious when our attention is focused on a complex situation; "Temporal confusion"—confusion over when things occur in time; and "Neuroplasticity"—our brains ability to change.

Inattentional Blindness

Studies show that if we're not paying attention to something, then we are less likely to see it. Daniel Simmons made a video, *the Monkey Business,* and used it to demonstrate the general inattentional blindness of most people. What Simmons showed was that inattentional blindness is not unusual—it is the norm. If you don't expect to see something, even if it is there in front of you, it may not register on your consciousness.

> STILL, A MAN HEARS WHAT HE WANTS TO HEAR & DISREGARDS THE REST.
> *Simon & Garfunkle*
> *The Boxer*

The Path of Imagination

> Only those items which I notice shape my mind—without selective interest, experience is an utter chaos. Interest alone gives accent and emphasis, light and shade, background and foreground—intelligible perspective, in a word.
>
> ~William James, The Principles of Psychology, (1890)

Worse than being blind is that we don't know we're blind. This can lead us to drive and talk on the cell phone at the same time. If we only knew how truly inattentionally blind we are, we would put that phone in the car trunk!

Imagine interviewing twelve people about a crime scene. Do you think they were all focused on the same things when the crime occurred? How many different stories might you get? Could people disagree about the basic "facts" of what happened?

Now remember the last time you got into an argument with someone about a difference of memory. You were certain they were wrong. But is it possible that your attention was simply focused differently? Perhaps one or both of you were inattentionally blind.

Inattentional blindness explains why long-time married couples can argue over the details of an event endlessly! Unexpected yet obvious things are often completely missed by otherwise competent humans. We are consciously aware of only a small portion of the immense amount of data bombarding our senses.

How to Create Abundance

Temporal Confusion

We interpret sounds, sights, smells, how something feels or tastes—and our thoughts—with our brain. And neuroscience has shown that our brain processes different sensory input at different times, at different rates of speed, and that tends to cause confusion.

> THE WORLD WE HAVE CREATED IS A PRODUCT OF OUR THINKING; IT CANNOT BE CHANGED WITHOUT CHANGING OUR THINKING.
>
> Albert Einstein

Researchers tried the following experiment. They had test subjects (students) press a button to make a bell ring. Gradually, over many repetitions, they slowed the time between the pressing of the button and when the ringing of the bell could be heard by the student. When they removed the artificial delay, the test subjects did not believe that they had caused the bell to ring.

The students had become used to the delay because their brain had adjusted their perception of the incoming sensory information, confusing them into thinking that they could not possibly have been the cause of the ringing bell because it happened faster than their perception had adjusted to. They were truly shocked and couldn't believe they'd caused the noise!

Another example of temporal confusion is the "80-millisecond rule." You can try this on your own. Stand 30 meters, or about 98 feet away from your friend and ask them to clap their hands together. Nothing strange happens. But just one step farther away—beyond 80 miliseconds traveling time for sound—you no longer see and hear the clap at the same time. The 80-millisecond rule demonstrates that sight and sound are not synchronized beyond 80 milliseconds. When sight and sound aren't in sync it's like watching that bad, late-night

The Path of Imagination

movie, or poorly edited YouTube video where the voice lags behind the lips forming the words.

Neuroplasticity

In addition to processing sensory information at different times. our brains might mix up our senses. While most of us don't taste color or see music, there are people who do. They have a condition called *synesthesia* that intermingles senses. Some synesthetics even have perfect pitch because their ability to see/hear color helps them discern notes.

The term neuroplasticity refers to our brains plastic and changeable nature. When we are injured, our brains can even form new neural connections—brains can "rewire." When our brains recognize something missing, we can "fill it in," but sometimes our brains fill in the missing sensory details by substituting the wrong information.

We misperceive the world around us. We can't help it. It's how we're made. Scientists and spiritual thinkers agree that most of the emotions that disturb us have incorrect perception as their basis.

IS THOUGHT A SENSATION?

What is thought and how is it the same or different from our senses of hearing, seeing, smelling, tasting, and touching? Is thought a sense?

EXERCISE IV

Dreams

Spend 5 minutes writing a eulogy for your life. Make sure to give yourself credit for all of your accomplishments.

Are there any dreams you have left unfulfilled?

How to Create Abundance

Like hearing, seeing, smelling, tasting, or touching, thought allows us to perceive and interact with the external world. People who survive without sensory input create their own worlds, just as dreamers create their own dreamworld.

Thought was viewed by the ancient Egyptians, and by some today, as simply another sense, and perhaps not the most important one.

> YOU ARE NOT A DROP IN THE OCEAN, YOU ARE THE ENTIRE OCEAN IN A DROP.
> Rumi

Who smells the flower, who sees the sky, who thinks the thought? We are not our senses, we are not our thoughts. Instead, our thoughts and senses are our vehicles for traveling the universe, for experiencing life. In this regard, you choose what to think just as you choose what to taste, touch, or look at. You can spit out things that taste unpleasant; you can look away from ugly sights; and *if you don't like the thought you are thinking,* you can think another.

THOUGHT & EMOTION

If thought is a sense, like taste and touch, then what is an emotion? Nobody really knows.

Because thought is present before emotion is experienced, many researchers believe thought creates emotion. Perhaps all senses have the ability to create emotion. Gazing at a beautiful sunset can make you feel awe, hearing certain music can make you feel sadness, and thinking certain thoughts can make you angry.

Western science has traditionally viewed thinking and emotion as completely separate. But at the end of the 20th century, researchers began studying the ways that thought and emotion are coded biologically—how thought and emo-

The Path of Imagination

tion turn into chemical information that together effect our bodies.

Our view of the world may be inaccurate due to faulty sensory perception that can lead to a difference between appearance and reality. Additionally, our emotions may be inaccurate in the context of what we experience. We may respond emotionally based on our beliefs rather than our present circumstances. Our beliefs are based on our thoughts which are based largely on what we were taught to think and believe when we were young, and may not reflect how we really feel now.

"S/he makes me so mad!" We've all thought it and said it. Yet no situation causes anger; the emotional reaction we had to our thought was anger. First there is the thought, and then the emotional response to the thought, because the thought is present before the emotion is felt. What are you thinking? How does that thought make you feel? If the answer is "not good," then change the thought.

To increase accurate perception, ask yourself:

1. *What emotions am I feeling now?*
2. *What thoughts created them?*

> WE SUFFER MORE OFTEN IN IMAGINATION THAN IN REALITY.
> Seneca the Younger

Negativity can be measured. The negative emotional response to the thought released cortisol into your bloodstream and contributed to your fight/flight response—you wanted to confront or disappear. When you couldn't do either, you became anxious as your body churned with unused adrenalin. Remember that discomfort?

How to Create Abundance

Now, imagine the opposite, perhaps the joy of greeting someone special after a long absence, or winning at sports. Positive thinking releases endorphins, the feel good hormones. The more positive thoughts you think, the better you'll feel!

Our body responds to our emotions by releasing chemicals like endorphins and cortisol. Our physical response gives us a gauge, a way to measure our emotional response to what we experience through our senses.

BELIEVE YOUR INTENTIONS ARE REAL

Just as we're not quite sure what "thinking" is, and we understand even less about "emotion," science is just beginning to map out what "intention" is and how it works. Researchers are asking questions like:

- Why do we see some things and are blind to other things?
- How much of our environment is recorded in our conscious or subconscious?
- How do we access information that is only available to our subconscious?

The answers to these questions will help us understand the nature of intention.

Researchers at the University of Waterloo, Canada report that "intention ties together biologically plausible mechanisms for belief, planning, and motor control." Intention has been studied since the 1950s and is of growing importance in neuroscience. It is important because scien-

WE DON'T GET WHAT WE WANT, WE GET WHAT WE BELIEVE.

Kelly Rosen

The Path of Imagination

tists need to understand how intention works so they can create working artificial limbs—for example, fingers we intend to pick things up with—to aid paralyzed patients. And it's important for lawyers to understand intention. There is a different punishment if you didn't *intend* to do something illegal. For these, and other reasons, intention is a hot topic.

Whether we create a cake, a book, or a friendship each of these creations begins with an intention. Each intention requires conviction—it requires the belief that we can actualize our intention and make it real. We create each moment of our lives by intending.

Tony Burroughs, author of *The Intenders of the Highest Good*, advises: "act like you've just ordered a pizza, and forget about it!"

"You don't worry that they might burn the crust, or, worse yet, put on some of those nasty anchovies that make you so sick to your stomach... The pizza place wants you to be happy. They're not out to get you... Likewise, the Universe desires to be our friend. It is we who sit and dwell on anchovies and burnt crust. We bring these undesired things to ourselves... If we concentrate our thoughts on problems, that's what

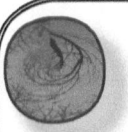

INTENTIONS EXPERIMENT IV

Intend Something Big

Spend a few minutes writing an intention that you hold dear, something big, something you might have been thinking of for years but have never acted on. Something you may have trouble believing can come true.

Use positive, present, and specific language. Read it every day, but don't ruminate over it. Simply read the statement one time per day and then go about your business. Just like you would after ordering a pizza!

How to Create Abundance

we'll get. Or, if we concentrate our thoughts on beneficence, that's what we'll get. Whatever it is that we concentrate our thoughts on, that's what we'll get."

Waiting patiently for a pizza is an act of conviction. You believe the pizza will arrive as ordered, and it does. If you can imagine it, and believe your imaginings, you have a better tool for getting what you want than the strongest will-power you can muster.

 WRITING for SELF DETERMINATION
ASSIGNMENT IV Beliefs

Write down three things that you believe in strongly. Now answer the following questions about your beliefs:

1. Where did the belief come from?
2. How has your thinking changed about it over time?
3. Is the belief helpful in achieving your goals?
4. Can the belief now be changed?

- _____
- _____
- _____
- _____
- _____
- _____
- _____
- _____
- _____
- _____

There is nothing more important to true growth than realizing that you are not the voice of the mind—you are the one who hears it.

~Adyashanti, *Falling Into Grace*

The person who risks nothing, does nothing, has nothing, is nothing, and becomes nothing. He may avoid suffering and sorrow, but he simply cannot learn & feel and change & grow and love & live.

Leo F. Buscaglia, "Born for Love"

Chapter 5

THE ROCK IN THE PATH

We walk the path created by our thinking. It would be best if we walked this path awake and aware to avoid obstacles and to get where we want to go in the most pleasant manner. Yet, we're motivated by our subconscious as well as our conscious intentions.

Your subconscious mind does not know the difference between what is real and what you imagine. It cannot distinguish between your waking desires, your dreams, and daydreams.

Your conscious mind is reading these words now. Your subconscious mind may be absorbing the content of a conversation unrelated to you going on in the same room, or reminding you of your fear of sitting in the dentist's chair in a few minutes, or your interest in that attractive stranger nearby. Your subconscious mind is absorbing all of the things around you and may populate your dreams with these tonight.

If you dream of making love, your body responds with a flood of hormones. If you dream of being chased, your body responds just as if you were, in fact, running—you wake with a racing heart and sweaty palms. This is because there is only one reality for the subconscious mind. It responds to memories and imaginings as if they were current and real.

How to Create Abundance

THE SHADOW KNOWS

"Who knows what evil lurks in the hearts of man?" asked the announcer of a 1939 radio show. The answer: "The Shadow knows" and it impacts our life in more ways than we can imagine.

People are often surprised by their subconscious—their shadow side. When their shadow makes an appearance they can only deny, "it wasn't me!" But our shadow is a part of us, a part that needs to be brought into the light for better viewing. Our shadow may prompt us to say or do things that seem to be out of character, "I don't know why I did that," or "I'm not normally like this."

When things happen that we don't want, we're manifesting from our shadow. When we're unaware of our subconscious desires, we may attract just exactly what we say we don't want. We deny, disown, alter, or project onto others rather than examining how we really feel. We can stuff our emotions down into the shadow, where we might pretend they no longer exist. We can use food, drugs, gambling, sex, etc. in order to continue to deny, and numb ourselves to what we know is true.

For example, someone says they want to become a supervisor at work. But they begin to suffer minor headaches and other health problems that keep them home and make their

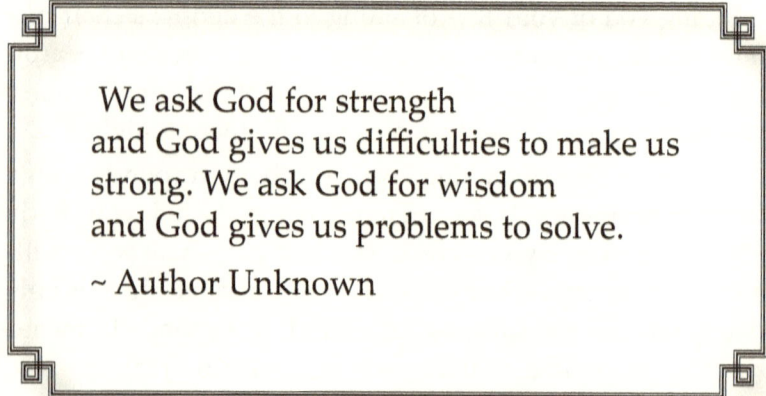

We ask God for strength
and God gives us difficulties to make us
strong. We ask God for wisdom
and God gives us problems to solve.

~ Author Unknown

promotion less likely. Consciously, they believe they want the responsibility of supervising others. Subconsciously, they fear leadership and have devised a way out! They lack awareness of their fear, and so determine that other people are preventing them from moving up at work.

People often project negative traits/wounds onto others. These are our blind spots. We next blame those others for the faults we've projected onto them. This is why religious teachings say it's best to pluck the crud from your own eye before you attempt to dig it out of anothers'—the crud in your own eye is blinding you!

Carl Jung, founder of analytical psychology, described how we project our shadow onto others. We bury what parents/society have taught us is negative, and then see it outside of us, instead of within.

When we recognize that others are our mirrors, we can reclaim our shadow and the power it holds. (A witch is powerful; a nice person is not so powerful.)

Although our shadow may seem unfathomable—like a fun house with wavy mirrors, or a deep, dark sea—Jung believed we could fish in the sea of unconsciousness for enlightenment and healing. But first we need to understand how the shadow works.

SEEKING THE SHADOW

We each have three brains, according to biologists, that have evolved over a very long time. The earliest is the reptilian brain used for self-preservation and our fight/flight response; next is the mammalian brain, used for nurturing and our emotional hub, and finally the cortex, the most recent part of our brain used for complex thinking.

The cortex takes a long time to reach maturity. That's why human babies don't just pop out and crawl away to take care of themselves like lizard, snake, or other reptile babies. Before the age of about three in humans, the reptilian brain and the

How to Create Abundance

mammalian brain are working just fine, but the cortex is undeveloped. Our fight/flight response is fully functional and our emotions are turned on and running full speed ahead, but the cortex—sorting it all out logically—isn't working yet.

Our "new brain" (the cortex) is associated with conscious thinking. Our "old brain" (the reptilian/mammalian) is associated with the subconscious. The new brain is rational. The old brain is irrational. Our new brain only works about 18 hours a day. Our old brain works twenty-four hours a day every day. The new brain controls our thinking, but the old brain controls our breathing and other automatic responses.

The conscious mind has a limited memory, the subconscious seems to be unlimited in its ability to remember even tiny, inconsequential details. The subconscious mind knows if someone is lying, even when the conscious mind believes. The subconscious mind knows when someone is looking at us, even when we don't see them. The conscious mind may ignore the sensation, but ignoring the subconscious mind is to our detriment.

According to Harry W. Carpenter author of, *The Genie Within*, "the conscious mind has the will and the subconscious mind has the power. When the conscious mind and the subconscious mind are in harmony, you have will-power. 'You are single minded.'"

To be single-minded is to be aware of your subconscious (your shadow), to harness its power, and then to act consciously to create the life you desire. We are single-minded when we decide with *both* our subconscious emotional mind, *and* our conscious thinking mind.

THE WORLD IS YOUR MIRROR

How do you bring what is subconscious into the light of day? Although it may be uncomfortable, when you face the shadow lurking inside, you can become single-minded... but you have to be willing to get to know yourself.

To identify your shadow self, take a look in the mirror that other people provide for you. A great place to seek the shadow is to examine what you like or dislike about others. What you admire in another, and those things you detest in others, often reflect your shadow side. They can mirror back to you what you cannot see in yourself.

You may have disowned positive traits that you admire in your friends just as you may have disowned your flaws, unable to see them in yourself. Yet, you are bothered by them when you see them in others.

We can also find our shadow in mistakes—in accidents and omissions. "Oops, sorry!" may reflect the deliberate action of the shadow. Have you left any trails of boo-boos? Can you identify any patterns of behavior? When one person complains, maybe it's just them; when several complain, maybe it's your shadow.

HARNESS THE SUBCONSCIOUS

Shadow work means digging in the dirt, ruffling through the rejected. Rather than sweeping the dirt back under the rug, we explore the things we find offensive, we dust off old ideas we thought were stupid (but might actually like), and select consciously what to accept and reject. Being a witch occasionally accomplishes goals that being nice doesn't. We can mine the shadow for ideas, power, and joy.

When we're able to look deep into our emotions and face our shadow, we come to the heart of our thinking. Writer

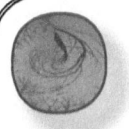

INTENTIONS EXPERIMENT V
The Mirror

Everything you see—character of friends, experiences—mirrors who you are. Notice what you like and don't like.

How to Create Abundance

Ruth Miller, PhD, says the underlying feeling—the trigger—is the language of our subconscious. The "surface thought" is our conscious response. These may be in conflict. Miller points out, "if you've been telling yourself how wonderful life is (surface thought), but your stored memories and initial feelings are full of dread and distress, the stuff of our universe is going to respond more immediately to the deeper feelings and memories than to the surface thoughts." In other words, emotion and thinking are at odds, and you are not single-minded.

When we harness our subconscious and act single-mindedly, the world is our oyster. It seems easy to achieve our dreams; people think we're lucky. When we subconsciously sabotage our intentions, we don't get anywhere—we spin our wheels. Or we go somewhere we don't want.

We can find ourselves "stuck" in our thinking and that makes us literally stuck in a reality we say we don't want. To be single-minded, our conscious and unconscious desires must be in harmony. We can find this harmony by harnessing the insight of the shadow. (*See list of 5 Steps To Lighten Your Shadow in Appendix D.*)

When we take deliberate steps toward our fear and act in spite of our fear—in spite of the voice within that says, "No!"—then we grow. Every time I sit down to write, there is a little voice inside of me that says, "Why don't you go do something better with your time?" It takes practice and persistence to ignore that voice and continue living the life *I* choose.

If you're not sure of your intention, or how to pursue your intention, then sleep on it. When you sleep on it, you give your subconscious mind an opportunity to communicate with you. You might be inspired upon arising.

Researchers at the University of Amsterdam have demonstrated that we're better at solving simple problems with our conscious mind. But when problems are more complex, our subconscious mind may be better at unravelling things and finding solutions. Sleep gives us a chance to sort it all out at a deeper level.

THE ROCK IN THE PATH

Have you ever tried to "push it" and have "it" backfire on you? Have you ever met resistance when you tried to force something or someone? What energy is preventing you from attaining your goals? Should you give up?

Some people think, "It's just not meant to be," but not many things can be achieved without meeting some resistance somewhere along the way. Persistence and tenacity are both important skills to develop in order to manifest your dreams.

However, persistence and tenacity sometimes fail, especially if the rock in our path is caused by our shadow. We may try and try, and feel as though we're just bashing our head against a wall.

If there is a boulder in front of you, tenacity and persistence might prompt you to grab a sledge-hammer and go at it. But some boulders are really large and indestructible except by eons of erosion, and you may be engaging in an act of futility.

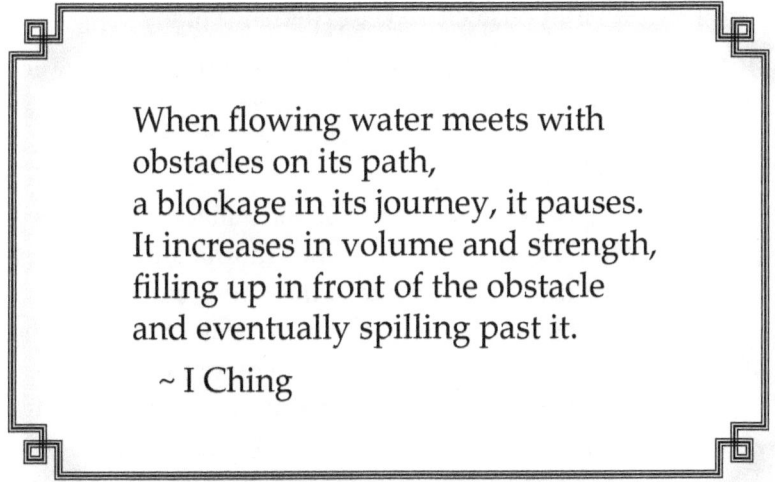

> When flowing water meets with obstacles on its path,
> a blockage in its journey, it pauses.
> It increases in volume and strength,
> filling up in front of the obstacle
> and eventually spilling past it.
>   ~ I Ching

How to Create Abundance

Stop and consider the situation from a broader perspective. First, examine your environment. What space are you trying to change, and what does the past, present and future of that space look like? If you can't move the boulder, can you get around it? Notice the flow of water around a rock in a fast-moving river. The water wears the rock down, and over time, turns it to pebbles and washes it to shore. Be like water when your dreams are blocked. Remain flexible, and keep in mind that intentions operate in their own time and way.

KNOW YOUR ENEMIES

In *The Teachings of Don Juan: A Yaqui Way of Knowledge,* by Carlos Castaneda, the author outlines four enemies, or obstacles we all must face on our path through life. These are the "rocks" that we may stumble upon:

FEAR. The 1st enemy to living a life of conscious choice—a big part of our shadow—is fear. Getting beyond fear is an important step on the journey of creating an abundantly fulfilled life.

CLARITY. The 2nd enemy is clarity—too much focus, or a limited perception. Clarity can prevent us from seeing in a different way, it can narrow our vision.

POWER. The 3rd enemy is power. Power can blind us to our vision. It can be an obstacle to the experience of joy.

OLD AGE. The 4th enemy is old age. By the time we conquer the first three enemies, we may be nearing the end of our lives.

FACE YOUR FEARS

The enemy of fear twists our already inaccurate perception, and leads us off course and into thorns and brambles. In order to avoid our fears, we take the wrong turn, we go in circles, or we remain motionless. We can make a tiny pebble in the road into a giant boulder we can't seem to get around.

Fear is an act of self-deception that we learn when we are young. You may deceive yourself into being afraid to achieve

The Rock in the Path

your dreams. You were not born afraid—not even of spiders and snakes. You were taught to fear by both non-verbal cues like facial expressions of anxiety, and words like "be careful!" And through smell. Mothers emit an odor—the odor of fear—and teach their babies to fear what they fear, even if their fear is irrational. The smell of fear is being studied by researchers at the University of Michigan.

Healthy fear is smart and respectful—it is healthy fear to get out of the way of a poisonous spider or a striking snake. It is not so healthy to spend time imagining a negative future or worrying about the past, yet many people spend a lot of time focused on irrational fear.

TECHNIQUES FOR DEALING WITH FEAR

We typically avoid what we fear. Instead, identify it and allow yourself to feel it. Get specific as you consider what you are afraid of. Is it a real threat or only imagined? What exactly is the worst that could happen? Are there any benefits that could come of the situation?

Fear must be faced, felt, and acknowledged. Naming the fear can remove the fear because acknowledgement brings knowing, and knowledge broadens our choices by changing our perception. As we learn, we think about things differently.

When you examine your fear, you will recognize that it's based in your thinking. You have the power to change your thinking. But it can be very difficult to

> FEAR IS THE PATH TO THE DARK SIDE. FEAR LEADS TO ANGER; ANGER LEADS TO HATE, HATE LEADS TO SUFFERING.
> *Yoda*

EXERCISE V
KNOW YOUR ENEMIES

We can learn how to face our internal enemies with assistance from our allies: Humility, Honesty, Harmony, & Humor
*Excerpted from writings about
Native American Traditional Teachings*

FIRST ENEMY: FEAR (Ally is Bliss found in Humility)

Confront the unknown. Face Fear by looking deep with self-love and self-acceptance; the enemy is defeated by "staying-in-the-now." Know Fear by knowing its opposite—Humility.

SECOND ENEMY: CLARITY (Ally is Honesty)

Confront your "truth." We tend to only see whatever symbols verify our view of our world. Face Clarity by opening to broader views; the enemy is defeated by acknowledging that there are many truths. Know Clarity by knowing its opposite—Honesty.

THIRD ENEMY: POWER (Ally is Compassion)

Confront your "karma." We tend to see Karma as a debt instead of as a teaching. Face Power by acomplishing for others; the enemy is defeated by sharing. Know Power by knowing its opposite—Compassion.

FOURTH ENEMY: OLD AGE (Ally is Humor)

Confront the process of your life's movement toward death. We don't wish to look at the fact that death gives life, and change is inevitable. Face Old Age by finding your sense of humor; the enemy is defeated by refusing to take ourselves seriously. Know Death by knowing its opposite—humor.

* It may seem strange that Death & Humor could be opposites. But it was reported in the Science Daily article, "People show more humorous creativity when primed with thoughts of death," that "humor helps the individual to tolerate latent anxiety that may otherwise be destabilizing." Humor has been shown to create resilience.

The Rock in the Path

acknowledge our fear, especially if it is an irrational fear from childhood. Sometimes, instead of facing our fear, we disown it and project it onto others and it becomes part of our shadow.

By accepting fear completely, without evading its cause or trying to escape the sensation, we come to the other side of our fear.

WHY INTENTIONS FAIL

When our conscious and subconscious intentions work together, we are single-minded. But when they do not act in unison, we may sabotage ourselves and act against our best interest.

When we hit a rock in the path, we have choices—we can give up or we can try to push through with persistence and tenacity. We can also examine our shadow to determine if we created the obstacle, and we can examine our shadow to see what helpful tools might be available but unused.

One way to harness the power of our shadow is to gain control over how our body responds to our thoughts and emotions. Think about the stress of driving in traffic and your neck stiffens. Think about a fuzzy kitten and your shoulders relax. We can learn to control our responses. When we mine

---

WRITING for SELF DETERMINATION
ASSIGNMENT V (a) Obstacles

Write your response to this question:

Where inside of me is the source of my anger, fear, frustration, joy, peace?

Don't ask *where outside of me is the source*...looking outside we see only distorted reflections. When we look inside, with honesty and courage, withholding judgement, we come to the source.

How to Create Abundance

our shadow for discarded power, we can achieve the single-mindedness needed to overcome the rock in our path.

To better understand how your shadow can impact, and even alter your intentions, consider the following questions:

1. Do the things that upset you a few years ago matter to you today?
2. Is it more important to do things right, or to do the right things?
3. Are you influencing your world, or is the world influencing you?
4. Which is worse: failing or never trying?
5. How old would you be if you didn't know how old you were?

Did you respond to any of these questions emotionally? Did you notice any ways your body responded? What thoughts underlie your responses? As you dig deeper, you could uncover surprises—our minds are interesting places to explore.

PUT YOUR THOUGHTS TO SLEEP, DO NOT LET THEM CAST A SHADOW OVER THE MOON OF YOUR HEART. LET GO OF THINKING.
Rumi

To go up into the light, you must go down into your darkness. To overcome your pain, you must first embrace it. To experience your power, you must feel your powerlessness. To realize your destiny, you must face your hopelessness. To arrive at the point of freedom, you must acknowledge the power of that which binds you... If you cannot find your pain, face it, feel it, and forgive it, you won't overcome it.

~ *Alan Mesher, The Silent Steps of Grace*

How to Create Abundance

WRITING for SELF DETERMINATION
ASSIGNMENT V (b) Fear

Spend a few minutes finishing each of the following sentences:

1. *If I had what I wanted right now, I'm afraid...*
2. *When I was younger I believed ___. Now I believe...*

I have
accepted fear
as part of life –
specifically the
fear of change...

I have gone ahead
despite the pounding in the heart that says:
turn back.

~ Erica Jong

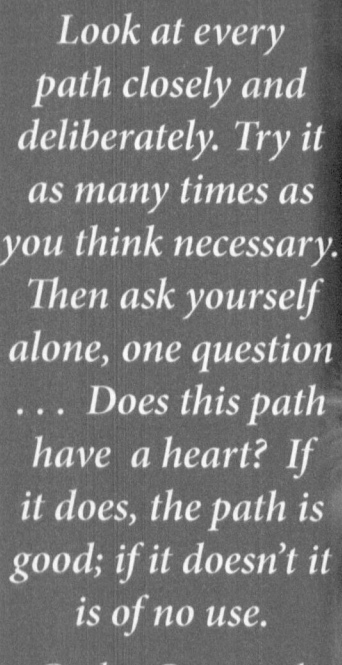

Look at every path closely and deliberately. Try it as many times as you think necessary. Then ask yourself alone, one question ... Does this path have a heart? If it does, the path is good; if it doesn't it is of no use.

~Carlos Castaneda, "The Teachings of Don Juan"

Chapter 6

THE PATH WITH HEART

People often admit "my heart wasn't really in it" when asked about their unmet desires. Those desires we are most likely to achieve are the ones we feel most strongly about. Strong emotion coupled with focused intention equals passion, and passion is powerfully creative. Passion is a product of the heart.

The heart and the brain both emit a strong electromagnetic field that can be detected and measured at a distance of several feet away from the body. And the heart and the brain are intrinsically connected. Researchers believe that the heart processes information and then communicates messages to the brain for further review.

Because the heart may respond to our environment before our brain can, our heart's intuition may lead us in the right direction faster and more directly than our cognitive thinking.

Our heart doesn't only "think"—receive and process messages internally—it communicates them externally. When we're feeling positive, the heart's electromagnetic field sends a different message than when we're feeling negative. Science is still studying how far this message can travel.

Sometimes we discover we are headed in the wrong direction—our hearts aren't in what we do—then it is time for a change of heart, or time to change directions. It doesn't mean

How to Create Abundance

that what we did in the past was wrong or wasted time, it simply isn't right for us now. It's time to adjust our sails (remember it takes only slight adjustments to make big changes), and head in a new direction.

GREAT INTENDERS

Some people are really good at making their dreams come true. They often shrug and say, "it's luck." But studies show there is more to it than luck.

There are some common characteristics of "lucky" people according to the Huffington Post article, *The Secrets Of The World's Luckiest People*. Lucky people tend to work hard quietly, surround themselves with positive people, put positive seeds into their minds every single day, fight overthinking, and have a clear purpose.

The "clear purpose" that lucky people demonstrate is a result of their passion—their heart is *into* what they are doing.

Lucky people are also grateful people. Research shows that people, who pay attention to what they are grateful for everyday, tend to reach their goals. Maybe this is because when we are grateful, our heart is into it—heart-felt emotions are involved.

WHAT'S HOLDING YOU BACK?

When we acknowledge what we are grateful for, it helps us overcome sensory desire. Sensory desire—sight, sound, taste, touch overload—is an obstacle to achieving mindfuless.

According to Buddhist tradition there are five obstacles to achieving mindfulness. These obstacles are: *sensory desire, ill-will, sloth, restlessness (or worry,)* and *doubt*.

In chapter one, we learned that practicing mindfulness can help us forgive ourselves and others, and lead to a happier, more fulfilled life.

INTENTIONS EXPERIMENT VI

What's Holding You Back?

Set an intention around one of the following: gratitude, compassion, courage, single-mindedness, or humility. Remember to use positive, present, and specific language.

THE FIVE OBSTACLES TO MINDFULNESS & HOW TO OVERCOME THEM

(as communicated in the Buddhist tradition):

1. Sensory desire: the type of wanting that seeks happiness through the five senses. (Overcome by practicing gratitude.)

2. Ill-will: thoughts of rejection; feelings of hostility, resentment, hatred, or bitterness. (Overcome by practicing flexibility/compassion.)

3. Sloth: "heaviness of body and dullness of mind which drag one down into disabling inertia and thick depression." (Overcome by developing fortitude/courage.)

4. Restlessness/worry: the inability to calm the mind. (Overcome by cultivating mindfulness and single-mindedness.)

5. Doubt: lack of conviction or trust. (Overcome by bliss found in humility.)

We overcome each obstacle by investigating it, understanding it, accepting its presence, and learning to deal with it. Occasionally, you can tell it to go away and it does; sometimes you have to allow it to exist before it dissipates.

~ Anson, Binh. *BuddhaSasana*

How to Create Abundance

We can overcome the five obstacles by getting to know them, and by practicing *gratitude, flexibility, physical fortitude, single-mindedness,* and *bliss.*

Practice Gratitude

Gratitude can be defined as that satisfying sense of thankfulness, sometimes mixed with relief, that connects us with others.

Gratitude is a special sort of emotion. It does *not* feel like obligation or indebtedness; if it did we might want to avoid our benefactor. Instead, the emotion of gratitude makes us gravitate toward that person.

Gratitude is a big deal in the major religions of our world. And in the early 21st century, psychologists began to study gratitude and how it motivates us. Psychologists have even come up with an "Appreciation Scale" to measure one's gratefulness level.

Research studies conducted by Robert Emmons of UC Berkley and others, show that "participants who kept gratitude lists were more likely to have made progress toward important personal goals." In addition to achieving their intentions, studies have shown that grateful people are happier, suffer less depression, and sleep better.

EXERCISE VI
APPRECIATION EXERCISE

Make a list of 10 things you are grateful for and why. Post the list where you can see it and review it regularly. Add one new item to your list each week.

The Path With Heart

In general, people who are the most grateful feel the best. This confirms the assertion in chapter one—you can't hold both a positive and a negative thought in your mind at the same time. If you are focused on gratefulness, you simply can't experience other negative emotions, especially resentment, at the same time.

Practice Flexibility

Flexibility is a requirement for effective intending; specifically flexible thinking. Our mind needs to be open about the possibility of our intention, open about just how the intention will be achieved, and open about the exact time and circumstances.

One particular experience helped my friend understand the need for remaining flexibly open to possibility. He had a home office with two high back, Queen Ann chairs that had seen better days. The material was faded and worn, the wooden legs were scratched, and the chairs were very uncomfortable. His wife really wanted them gone. He was worried that if he got rid of the chairs, he'd have no seating in his office and wanted to wait until he'd found suitable replacements. His wife worried that it might be a long time before they were replaced.

I told them about the concept of "holding the empty space." This is it in a nutshell: Clear the space of what you don't want, including your mind space of what you don't want. Next, contemplate this empty space unemotionally, let it settle with you. Finally, envision the empty space filled in just the way you desire.

My friend agreed to remove the ugly chairs temporarily, allowing empty space in his office. A few days later, while driving his daughter to school, he saw two beautiful chairs sitting near the curb, removed from a local business for a remodel. The chairs were in great condition: clean—unblemished material in a nice blue color—with polished wood legs,

How to Create Abundance

and very comfortable. Imagine his joy when he placed the new chairs in his office, filling the space exactly as he'd pictured it in his mind.

Practice Physical Fortitude

"Stand up straight," children are told. This is good advice for healthy posture, and it also positively effects the way we think.

According to Ian H. Robertson in his book, *The Winner Effect*, one way we can change our beliefs is to pay attention to our posture, "Even tiny, short-lasting changes in the way we hold ourselves can change our bodies and brains in profound ways. No wonder parents urge their adolescents not to slump."

Just as putting on a suit and tie makes many people involuntarily stand up taller, standing up straight and tall may make people involuntarily more confident. So, if you are feeling that your dreams are blocked, don't sit. Stand!

Physical fortitude also involves "putting your best foot forward" (a colloquial phrase meaning to "embark on a journey or task with purpose and gusto).”

Hardiness and fortitude are synonyms. They are defined similarly as: the "strength of mind that enables a person to encounter danger or bear pain or adversity with courage," and "capable of withstanding adverse conditions." —Webster online dictionary.

Salvatore Maddi, founder of the Hardiness Institute, and his team of researchers

> "STAND. IN THE END YOU'LL STILL BE YOU, ONE THAT'S DONE ALL THE THINGS YOU SET OUT TO DO,"
> *Sly and the Family Stone*

The Path With Heart

FIRST YOU MAKE YOUR BELIEFS, & THEN YOUR BELIEFS MAKE YOU.
Marisa Peer

at the University of Chicago define hardiness as: "a combination of three attitudes (commitment, control, and challenge) that together provide the courage and motivation needed to turn stressful circumstances from potential calamities into opportunities for personal growth."

On his website, Maddi provides a hardiness questionnaire, The HardiSurvey®, to help people discover their hardiness quotient. This is a test of, "stress management and coping resilience" that "evaluates individual and organizational resources for effectively managing stressful changes."

People can develop fortitude and become skilled at hardiness. It just takes some practice. Maddi thinks increasing hardiness will lead to a more fulfilling life.

Practice Single-Mindedness

We are single-minded when we harness the power of the subconscious and then act consciously to create the life we desire. We are single-minded when we listen to our heart and make our decisions with our spirit as opposed to our thinking minds alone. Ask yourself, *"is my heart really in this?"*

We are single-minded when we are compassionate with others, as opposed to feeling just intellectual sympathy for someone. Dr. Phillipe Goldin asserts in *The Neuroscience of Emotions*, that compassion is both cognitive—part of our thinking process—and emotional. Goldin defines compassion as: "The deep awareness of the suffering of another person coupled with the wish, the intention, the motivation to relieve that person from their suffering. So it's both an emotional component and a cognitive component."

How to Create Abundance

We are single-minded when we are compassionate with ourselves. "Be gentle with yourself," Max Ehrmann recommended in *Desiderata*.

When we practice compassion, we adjust our perception. In chapter 4 we saw that most of the emotions that disturb us have incorrect perception as their basis—there is a gap between appearance and reality. If we can view something from a different angle, our perception shifts. One way to correct our misperceptions is by practicing compassion. Recent research shows practicing compassion helps us perceive more accurately, according to Melissa Donaldson from the online magazine, *6 Seconds*.

Follow Your Bliss

"Follow your bliss" means to follow the path of true desire. When you follow your bliss you spend time in ways that make you forget time altogether. You get into the "zone." The Urban Dictionary defines "in the zone" as: "Being com-

---

Each of us is born with a treasure, an essence, a seed of quiescent potential, secreted for safekeeping in the center of our being. This treasure, this personal quality, power, talent, or gift (or set of such qualities), is ours to develop, embody, and offer to our communities in acts of service—our contributions to a more diverse, vital, and evolved world. Our personal destiny is to become that treasure through our actions.

~ Jason Kirkey, The Salmon in Spring: The Ecology of Celtic Spirituality.

pletely unaware of what's going on around you as you are so extremely into what's going on right in front of your face."

Mythographer Joseph Campbell talked to his graduate students at Sarah Lawrence College about bliss. He said, "If you do follow your bliss you put yourself on a kind of track that has been there all the while, waiting for you, and the life that you ought to be living is the one you are living. When you can see that, you begin to meet people who are in the field of your bliss, and they open the doors to you."

When we learn to deal with our *sensory desire, ill-will, sloth, worry,* and *doubt* we overcome the obstacles to mindfulness, and come to a place of acceptance—accepting ourself and others.

By following your heart—your bliss—you will free yourself to discover the path that leads to a mindful life.

SET YOUR LIFE ON FIRE. SEEK THOSE WHO FAN YOUR FLAMES.

Rumi

How to Create Abundance

 WRITING for SELF DETERMINATION

ASSIGNMENT VI Gratefullness

Practicing gratefulness isn't always easy.
Here are some ideas to get started:

1. Come into the present moment. As Ram Das says, "be here now." Focus on your senses. What do you hear now? What do you see now? What are you touching now? As you settle into the present moment, consider, "what am I grateful for now?"

2. Find reasons to say, "thank you," and mean it.

3. Write a letter to someone expressing your gratitude for something they did or said. Now deliver it. This exercise creates happiness that research shows can last an entire month!

4. Keep a gratitude journal. It can help keep you happy indefinitely!

Beyond a wholesome discipline, be gentle with yourself. You are a child of the universe, no less than the trees and the stars; you have a right to be here. And whether or not it is clear to you, no doubt the universe is unfolding as it should. Therefore be at peace with God, whatever you conceive Him to be. And whatever your labors and aspirations in the noisy confusion of life, keep peace in your soul. With all its sham, drudgery, and broken dreams, it is still a beautiful world.

~ Max Ehrmann, *Desiderata*

A small group of thoughtful people could change the world. Indeed, it's the only thing that ever has.

~ Margaret Mead

Chapter 7

OUR COMMON PATH

What would our world be like without you? What people and events have changed simply due to your presence? What chain reactions have you caused or prevented?

Of course, you probably don't know how important you are. You may not be aware of the many times and many ways that your presence in our world has impacted people and events.

In the movie, *It's a Wonderful Life*, the leading man, Jimmy Stewart, declares: "I wish I'd never been born." His wish is granted by an angel who shows him exactly what the world would be like without him—a sadder and more desolate place—in order to help him understand the importance of his life to others.

Try to imagine the effect of your life upon another, and their effect on yet another, and so on. You may come to the realization that your presence has changed the world.

ENERGY, FREQUENCY, & VIBRATION

When we set intentions, we set things in motion. We set energy to vibrating, like humming a tune. The changes we intend, change others, too; they change our harmony together.

Early in the 20th century quantum physics was discovered and explored, and as scientists began to understand the

How to Create Abundance

quantum world, they came to realize the truth of what was written thousands of years ago in the ancient Vedic Texts (and emblazoned in poem by Walt Whitman): life is energy.

Physicist Nikola Tesla asserted, "The day science begins to study non-physical phenomena, it will make more progress in one decade than in all the previous centuries of its existence. To understand the true nature of the universe, one must think in terms of energy, frequency and vibration."

Energy, frequency, and vibration have to do with interaction. When you set intentions, you set energy in motion. Your actions send ripples out into the world. It really isn't possible to set intentions for yourself and not impact others. Every intention ultimately involves other people.

THE POWER OF ONE

Rosa Parks' bones ached and she was tired of standing up and giving her seat on the bus to younger people just because they were white. She was an ordinary person whose actions changed our world.

Anne Mahlum, an average woman who liked to run, started a running club for young men at a homeless shelter. That program eventually became the non-profit organization: "Back on My Feet" that helps people improve their education and find jobs. Their motto: "Changing lives one mile, job, and house at a time."

Anne Mahlum isn't famous, but like Rosa Parks, her actions created positive change in our world.

Changemakers are often unknown, but they aren't unusual. The internet is filled with stories of ordinary heros. One

> THERE IS A SENSE IN WHICH WE ARE ALL EACH OTHER'S CONSEQUENCES.
> *Wallace Stegner*

person's passion can ignite important and beneficial transformation in others, sometimes many others.

THE ABILITY TO RESPOND

We are responsible for our choices. The choice is up to us every moment to select carefully our next step on our journey. It is a narrow path that leads to a joyful life.

People who take responsibility, even if something isn't their fault, are changemakers. They improve our world.

The ability to respond, verses merely reacting (acting again/back to someone or something), is a powerful reflection of self-development.

When someone takes 100% responsibility for their thoughts and actions, amazing things can happen, synchronicities occur—like meeting the right person at just the right time. Rosa Parks and Anne Mahlum took responsibility—they were able to respond—and their responses ultimately led to positive change for many.

> *"Thus we come into relationships to mirror and reflect for one another. We are tools for each other's growth and the more we can truly know this, the faster the movement. There is no need for judgment of a particular relationship as right or wrong. Each relationship is merely the mirroring we need at a particular time for our highest good."*
>
> ~ Harley Swiftdear Reagan, Dear Tribe Metis-Medicine Society

How to Create Abundance

In the *Huffington Post article*, "3 Reasons Why Taking Responsibility Is Spiritual," Shakti Sutriasa recommends asking the following questions to help you decide if you're ready to take 100% responsibility:

1. Are you willing to own whatever happens in your life?
2. Can you discern between what you do and don't have control over? In other words, you only have control over you, and how you respond to life's challenges and opportunities. You do not have any control over what other people do or say.
3. Are you ready to be okay when you screw up and when you succeed?

Sutriasa asserts that taking responsibility for your life will transform it.

PRACTICE RESPONSIBILITY

People from different cultures and religions have different ways of developing the ability to respond. Here are three examples of traditional practices that some people follow to help them become more aware, forgiving, and responsible: *Insight meditation*, *Ho'oponopono*, and *Radical Affection*.

Insight Meditation

Insight meditation, or Vipassana, is an ancient system of training your mind, a set of exercises to help you become more aware of your own life experience. It is a gentle technique, but it is very thorough. It involves attentive listening, mindful seeing, and careful awareness.

> "Iktsuarpok:"
> "THE FEELING OF ANTICIPATION THAT LEADS YOU TO LOOK OUTSIDE TO SEE IF ANYONE IS COMING."
> an Inuit word
> *Hygge* by Meik Wiking

Insight meditation is concerned with the present moment—staying in the now to the most extreme degree possible. Bhante Henepola Gunaratana in *Tricycle Magazine*, states, "We learn to smell acutely, to touch fully, and to really pay attention to the changes taking place in all these experiences. We learn to listen to our own thoughts without being caught up in them."

> We think we are doing this already, but that is an illusion. It comes from the fact that we are paying so little attention to the ongoing surge of our own life experience that we might just as well be asleep. We are simply not paying enough attention to notice that we are not paying attention.

Ho'oponopono

Ho'oponopono (ho-o-pono-pono) means "to make right." It's based on the ancient Hawaiian practice of reconciliation and forgiveness. Informally, it is used in families to settle arguments and address disturbing thoughts—including those caused by dreams. The practice of Ho'oponopono is based on the belief that all past debts must be forgiven and released.

Practitioners of Ho'oponopono might use the mantra: "I'm sorry. Please forgive me. Thank you. I love you."

Many people in various cultures around the globe have believed that illness was caused by anger or disharmony, including bad feelings toward others in dreams. When I studied Medical Anthropology, I learned about the Achuar tribe of southeastern Ecuador who grow up respecting their dreams as an extension of their daily life. They work to re-

INTENTIONS EXPERIMENT VII

Write an intention for the world. The intention can be for the entire planet, or the people on it, or both. Use language that is positive, present, and specific.

How to Create Abundance

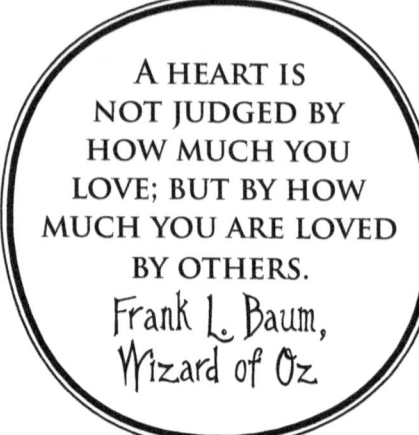

A HEART IS NOT JUDGED BY HOW MUCH YOU LOVE; BUT BY HOW MUCH YOU ARE LOVED BY OTHERS.
Frank L. Baum, Wizard of Oz

member their dreams, and share them with others. If they dream about harming another member of the tribe, they seek out that person, apologize and make amends as if they'd performed the discourtesy in their waking life.

Radical Affection

Radical Affection is based on the idea of accepting 100% responsibility regardless of situation or circumstances. You own and are responsible for the outcome of every experience you choose.

100% Responsibility, according to some, means that everything exists as a projection from inside the human being; you created the experience of being here now.

This view, though extreme, may be motivating and beneficial for some whose life circumstances appear to be out of their control—they may be motivated to take responsibility and gain control. However, this view may be unmovating for others. It is especially unmotivating if it stirs feelings of self-blame and/or resentment. Practicing Radical Affection can only be helpful if we've first mastered 100% forgiveness.

When we practice Radical Affection, we take complete responsibility for our life. Everything we see, hear, taste, touch, or in any way experience is our responsibility because it is part of our life. Any problem with our external reality, is really within ourselves. To change our reality, we have to change ourselves, specifically our choice of sensory experience and thinking.

THE POWER OF MANY

There are groups of people who regularly set intentions for others. For example, people who pray for others, people who practice Transcendental Meditation, members of the Changemakers organization, Tony Burroughs' intenders circle participants, and more.

> THE OPPOSITE OF ADDICTION IS NOT SOBRIETY. IT IS HUMAN CONNECTION.
> Johann Hari
> Chasing The Scream

Setting intentions with others can be very powerful, but you don't have to join a group to create a powerful chain reaction of positivity. Anybody can *Pay it Forward*!

PAY IT FORWARD

Have you ever stood in a canyon and shouted, "hello," and listened to the echoes reverberating around you? Mother Teresa said, "kind words can be short and easy to speak, but their echoes are truly endless."

Do you remember a time when you were in need, perhaps even desperate, and someone appeared and assisted you? They gave you something (perhaps a listening ear, or a shoulder to cry on), and they wanted nothing in return? The desire to pass this goodness on is commonly called "pay it forward."

The original use of the phrase, "pay it forward" probably came from this passage written in 1951:

> *The banker reached into the folds of his gown, pulled out a single credit note. 'But eat first—a full belly steadies the judgment. Do me the honor of accepting this as our welcome to the newcomer."*

How to Create Abundance

His pride said no; his stomach said YES. Don took it and said, "Uh, thanks! That's awfully kind of you. I'll pay it back first chance."

"Instead pay it forward to some other brother who needs it."

~ Robert Heinlien, *Between Planets.*

We create a ripple effect when we *Pay it forward,* just like a stone cast across the water, the energy magnifies. A smile at the right time to a person in need can change more than their day. They might pass it on to others, changing the world!

"Pay it forward" can become a phenomena. For example, a Florida Starbucks in August, 2014 had 750 generous customers who continued to buy the next customer coffee for two days!

EXERCISE VII
LAUGHING OUT LOUD

Try this experiment:

- Find a comfortable place where you can be as loud as you like and not disturb anyone or be disturbed.
- Relax your shoulders and arms and take a few deep breaths.
- Now laugh out loud. It's OK if it doesn't feel natural or if it sounds fake. Keep it up anyway. Laugh as loud and as long as you can.

(On our common path, laughter is best practiced in unison. It is not recommended to practice this activity alone in public!)

Our Common Path

How might you pay it forward? Consider the following questions:

1. What can I contribute?
2. What are my limitations?
3. Who can offer support?
4. Who can I support?
5. Where is the overall good created?

Facing fears, gaining control of negative thinking, learning to examine and detach from strong feelings, and learning how to generate positivity in the present moment are skills that help us overcome individual and collective problems.

As you learn to set broader, more insightful intentions, and begin to work with others to set community intentions, you are laying the foundation for a new road. By following your vision, you also become a guiding light for others. You are, in fact, a pioneer.

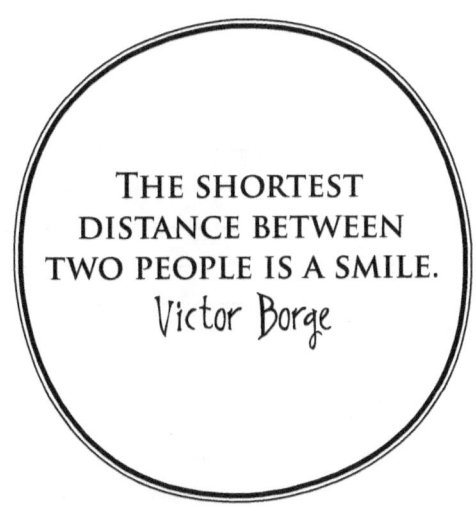

How to Create Abundance

WRITING for SELF DETERMINATION
ASSIGNMENT VII The Power of Many

Spend 10 minutes describing how you might pay it forward. Where would you start? A toll-booth? A restaurant? A movie theater? Give plenty of details about the location.

What will you give? Will you give money, like paying the toll behind you or buying desert for the next customer? Will you "pay forward" a book or other item? A smile?

What impact do you think your actions might have on others? Do you think others might join you and create a chain reaction? Is there some deeper, more meaningful pay it forward you can think of? Why not give it a try?

- _____
- _____
- _____
- _____
- _____
- _____
- _____
- _____
- _____
- _____
- _____
- _____
- _____
- _____
- _____
- _____
- _____
- _____

Each of us can bring a unique gift to the world, a world desperately in need of the socially transforming contributions of initiated, actively engaged adults. I hear the world itself calling for a renaissance of the human soul or, as James Hillman says, for a psyche the size of the earth.

~ Bill Plotkin, *Nature and the Human Soul*

The moment one definitely commits oneself, then providence moves too. All sorts of things occur to help one that would never otherwise have occurred... Unforeseen incidents, meetings, and material assistance, which no man could have dreamed would have come his way.

~Johann Wolfgang Von Goethe

Chapter 8

THE PATH OF TRANSFORMATION

Transformation may require an incubation process—a cocooning—but it happens all at once. After transformation occurs, there's no going back. You are on a new path.

We usually see transformation as positive, as something that leads to renewed possibility. It is defined as: "a thorough or dramatic change in form or appearance; synonyms include: change, alteration, mutation, conversion, metamorphosis, transfiguration, transmutation, sea change," according to *Google Online Dictionary*.

Transformational change is different from developmental change or transitional change. With developmental change, "we learn new things and grow, but our understanding of ourselves and the world that we are a part of has not necessarily changed," according to Jim Marsdon in his article, "A Journey of Transformation."

With transitional change, "we assess where we are today and where we would like to be in the future... then look at the gap between where we are now and where we'd like to be." Again, no world-altering understanding has occurred, Marsdon points out.

How to Create Abundance

Transformational change is different. It happens when "our foundational understanding of ourselves and the world around us significantly shifts. A transformation occurs when we go beyond the bounds of our current understanding and awareness. We cannot think our way through this change; we have to experience our way into it."

Perhaps one of the most significant transformations people report comes through acceptance—accepting the way they are and/or accepting the way other people are. With acceptance, we give up expecting the "ideal" and instead accept the human reality. As with any other transformation, we can't *will* acceptance with thought, we have to *experience* the change.

THE IDEAL

Greek philosopher, Plato, described "the ideal" as perfect and unattainable—the perfect flower that all other flowers are mere copies of; the perfect parent or hero that all other parents or heros only want to be.

This concept of "the ideal" was reaffirmed by physicist Sir Roger Penrose in his interpretation of quantum mechanics. According to Penrose, platonic constants, or "the ideal" is embedded in the structure of the universe, and within us. It lead us to "do the right thing" and to improve or evolve our consciousness over time as we stretch to reach the unachievable perfection of "Truth," "Beauty," and "Justice."

> "Cafune:"
> "THE ACT OF TENDERLY RUNNING ONE'S FINGERS THROUGH THE HAIR OF A LOVED ONE."
> a Brazilian word
> *Hygge* by Meik Wiking

Path of Transformation

According to the director of Harvard's Primate and Cognitive Neuroscience Laboratory, Marc Hauser, "the ideal" does exist within us.

His internet-based research study, called the Moral Sense Test, published a report in 2003 gauging the moral intuitions of people from all over the world.

The results of the "Moral Sense Test" support the theory that there is a "universally shared moral faculty" common to all human beings and rooted in our evolutionary heritage:

> *Every human culture has some sort of moral code, and these overlap to a considerable extent. There is a common core of shared values such as trustworthiness, friendship, and courage, along with certain prohibitions, such as those against murder or incest. Some version of the golden rule — treat others as you would have them treat you — is also encountered in almost every society.*

Trustworthiness, loyalty, courage, fortitude, honor, courtesy, sincerity, compassion, humility, and humor are qualities that define moral character for many different people in different places and times. Previous generations of Americans were taught that moral character was an important virtue and

---

"Although I am a typical loner in my daily life, my awareness of belonging to the invisible community of those who strive for truth, beauty, and justice has prevented me from feelings of isolation."

~ Albert Einstein

How to Create Abundance

were given instruction on how to develop character. Students were required to memorize poems that contained moral nuggets; inspirational character-building quotes from famous people filled popular books and pamphlets. Character was a topic of discussion.

> EASY CHOICES, HARD LIFE.
> HARD CHOICES, EASY LIFE.
> *Jerzy Gregbrek*

Today, some people find it hard to define and distinguish the terms: *ethics, morals, virtue,* and *character*.

Ethics: "refer to rules provided by an external source, e.g., codes of conduct in workplaces or principles in religions," *and*

Morals: "refer to an individual's own principles regarding right and wrong," as defined in *"Ethics vs Morals." Diffen.com.*

Virtue: "a quality considered morally good or desirable in a person," *as defined by the English Oxford Online Dictionary.*

Character: "the complex of mental and ethical traits marking and often individualizing a person, group, or nation: "the character of the American people," *as defined by the Merriam-Webster Online Dictionary.*

Character Building: "improving certain good or useful traits in a person's character, esp self-reliance, endurance, and courage," *as defined by the Collins Online Dictionary.*

The importance of character building was replaced in the early twentieth century by an emphasis on personality and personal fulfillment. The focus away from morality and toward personality helped to sell products, according to cultural historian Warren Susman who wrote about the rise and fall of the concept of character in his book, *Culture as History.*

Path of Transformation

According to Susman, books and publicatoins that, in the past, had focused on doing good works, started to focus on satisfying personal desires. "The vision of self-sacrifice began to yield to that of self-realization," Susman writes. But focusing on personal fulfillment did not lead to greater happiness. As we saw in chapter two, happiness comes from achieving difficult, long-term goals, not from possessing a new gadget.

CHARACTER vs PERSONALITY

Unlike personality, character is not merely personal tastes and preferences. Instead, character is something one develops over time. You may be born with personality, but you define and improve character through habits and intentions.

Possessing a strong character means you have a handle on your petty needs and wants; you not only tolerate difficult circumstances, but may choose life challenges—physical and mental—that help develop positive character traits and prevent negative character traits like sloth, restlessness and doubt.

According to H.S. Holland, "the single greatest influence on our character is that which we have ultimate power over: how we respond to circumstances. Writers of the 19th century agreed that the true exercise and test of a man's character was whether he would hold to his moral principles no matter how sorely tempted or how painful the repercussions."

YESTERDAY I WAS CLEVER, SO I WANTED TO CHANGE THE WORLD. TODAY I AM WISE, SO I AM CHANGING MYSELF.
Rumi

How to Create Abundance

HAPPY PEOPLE ARE ETHICAL PEOPLE

Happy people have a strong code of ethics that guide them. This is backed up by research conducted by economist Harvey S. James, and others. James discovered that ethical people tended to be more satisfied with life in general.

Researchers asked four ethics questions about the acceptability of: claiming government benefits to which you are not entitled, avoiding paying your fare on public transportation, cheating on taxes, and accepting a bribe.

The researchers also asked: "On a scale of 1 to 10, how satisfied are you with your life?"

The study concluded that people who behaved more ethically, also rated themselves more satisfied.

James explained in an interview with *Miller-McCune* staff writer, Tom Jacobs, "not being willing to justify ethically questionable behaviors may improve a person's psychological well-being, perhaps because he or she avoids feelings of guilt or shame. This could in turn produce an increase in happiness."

For happiness sake, strive for big character, and small personality!

"Character gains through its expression, and loses through its repression. Love grows through its expression. Sympathy grows through its expression. Knowledge grows through its expression. The artistic sense grows through its expression...

~ Henry Clay Trumbull, *Character-Shaping and Character-Showing*, 1894

Path of Transformation

EXERCISE YOUR CHARACTER

The path to an abundantly fulfilled life lies within each of us; it is within our control. We can develop our inner strengths and positive character traits and find true satisfaction through those efforts alone.

There are many ways to practice character building. For example, *Stoicism*. Stoicism comes from an ancient Greek philosophy and centers around a few teachings. Stoics acknowledge how unpredictable the world can be; they learn how to be steadfast, and strong, and in control of self; and they strive to leave the world better than they found it.

For Stoics, the source of unhappiness lies in, "our impulsive dependency on our reflexive senses." Stoicism provides a sort of mental-toughness training. It can be seen as a character building expedition according to the article, "What Is Stoicism?" *The Daily Stoic*.

"Stoicism doesn't concern itself with complicated theories about the world, but with helping us overcome destructive emotions and act on what can be acted upon."

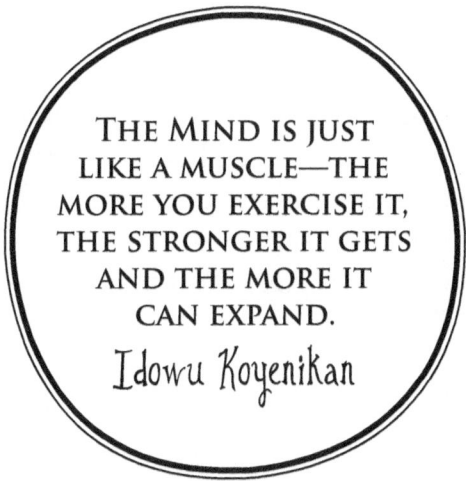

> THE MIND IS JUST LIKE A MUSCLE—THE MORE YOU EXERCISE IT, THE STRONGER IT GETS AND THE MORE IT CAN EXPAND.
>
> Idowu Koyenikan

How to Create Abundance

Here is one of the exercises *The Daily Stoic* recommends:

Turning the Obstacle Upside Down

Consider any obstacle. Now try to imagine all of the positive benefits the obstacle brings. This exercise makes it impossible to not practice the art of philosophy. If you can properly turn a problem upside down, every "bad" becomes a new source of "good."

Suppose for a second that you are trying to help someone and they respond by being surly or unwilling to cooperate. Instead of making your life more difficult, the exercise says they're actually directing you toward new virtues, for example, patience or understanding.

IDENTIFY YOUR VIRTUES

A path to a virtuous life is described by people in almost every culture. Most people, at different times in history, defined important principles like honesty, loyalty, courage, etc. Two examples we've looked at are the teachings of Buddhist monks on how they endeavored to overcome the obstacles to

> "Watch your thoughts, they become words; watch your words, they become actions; watch your actions, they become habits; watch your habits, they become character; watch your character, for it becomes your destiny."
>
> ~ Frank Outlaw

INTENTIONS EXPERIMENT VIII
SEVEN VIRTUES OF A WARRIOR

Cultivating Virtues

Set an intention around one of the following: courage, honor, coutesy, loyalty, honesty, sincerity, or compassion. Remember to use positive, present, and specific language.

From Native American Traditional Teachings exerpted from Swiftdeer in "Sacred Wheel Teachings"

1. COURAGE: Totally open and unlimited imagination which gives us artistic originality.
2. HONOR: deep introspection/intuition which gives us a true refinement of our character.
3. COURTESY: Complete trust/innocence which gives us the way to properly relate to those people who are in our immediate everyday environment.
4. LOYALTY: True wisdom/logic which gives the clarity and strength of mind to be spiritually awake.
5. HONESTY: open heart to heart communication with ourselves and others which helps us in our knowing our true identy.
6. SINCERITY: Accepting concepts of our self which guide us in our statements and viewpoints we make in relationship to general knowledge.
7. COMPASSION: Ability to completely open our symbols of the dream experience in order to know the connection we have to all forms of all things within the Everything.

Which Virtues have you developed?

Which enemies have you faced?

How to Create Abundance

mindfulness; and Native American teachings on how to use our allies of humility, honesty, harmony, and humor.

These universal principles are often expressed as a dichotomy (either/or) such as: courageous versus cowardly, humble versus vain, greedy versus charitable, etc. They create a paradox—a yin-yang juxtaposition—the yin seed lies within the yang; the yang seed lies within the yin.

Many cultures emphasize seven, or more, specific virtues. For example, there are seven Christian virtues: four classical cardinal virtues—prudence, justice, temperance and courage (or fortitude); and three theological virtues—faith, hope and charity.

In Native American tradition there are also seven virtues a warrior seeks to develop: courage, honor, courtesy, loyalty, honesty, sincerity, and compassion.

"The Way of the Warrior reminds us that we have a responsibility to live by a code of ethics that serves to help us reach a higher standard of living," according to Two Feathers, Kainaiwa Clan of the Blackfoot.

MEDICINE WALK

In Native American tradition a Medicine Walk is a kind of vision quest. It is a time spent in nature—an exploration of the open road like the one described by Whitman, an aimless wandering that may bring enlightenment.

Medicine is a type of power. It does not fix things for you, but it can assist you. It can be hard to swallow, even unpleasant. It is subtle, but can produce broad transformation.

This workbook is a type of guided Medicine Walk. It is meant to allow you to slow down, tune in, shift consciousness, and receive the medicine that your soul needs. You may wish to go back over it again and again. As Thoreau reminds us: "a single footstep will not make a path on the earth."

Path of Transformation

On your journey through this workbook—and through life—you are presented with many obstacles. The path you follow toward self-determination and control of your destiny is not without stumbling-stones, but there are allies and helpers along the way.

In chapter one you encountered the obstacle of negative thinking and ill-will, and learned techniques of forgiveness and thought control.

In chapter two you encountered the obstacle of desire, and learned to be loyal to the expectations of your higher self.

In chapter three you encountered the obstacle of doubt, and learned the language of magic—the difference between wishing and intending.

In chapter four you encountered the obstacle of narrow-vision, and learned to set clear-sighted intentions by discovering your blind-spots.

In chapter five you encountered the obstacle of fear, and learned single-mindedness.

In chapter six you encountered the obstacles to mindfulness, and learned the significance of gratitude.

In chapter seven, you encountered the obstacle of sloth, and learned the power and momentum of intention.

The next step is to face the obstacle of inflexibility, and accept the process of transformation.

May this workbook help you explore habits to cultivate, or prune, on the path to an abundantly fulfilled life.

LET GO OF WHO YOU ARE AND BECOME WHO YOU MIGHT BE.
Rumi

How to Create Abundance

We can look outside or inside. We can direct our intentions outside of ourselves to material acquisition and change of physical environment. Or, we can direct our attention and intention inside of ourselves to inner development and change. We can become skilled warriors in our own lives.

When we tend to the flowers growing within we begin to see a different landscape without. As Dorothy said in *The Wonderful Wizard of Oz*.:

> "If I ever go looking for my heart's desire again, I won't look any further than my own back yard. Because if it isn't there, I never really lost it to begin with."
>
> ~ L. Frank Baum,

THE BEAUTY WAY

The beauty way is a way of harmony. When our conscious and unconscious desires are in harmony, we are single-minded—we are aware of our subconscious shadow and able to harness its power. When we listen to our heart, and make our decisions with our spirit, as opposed to our thinking mind alone, we act mindfully.

To walk the Beauty Way we remember that every thought, word, and deed is an opportunity to reach for the ideal. It matters not if we attain the ideal; the effort is its own reward.

As we reach for the ideal in our thoughts, words, and deeds we leave a trail. The trail we create from our decision to choose beauty—to step here, and not there—becomes our path. Our path becomes our way. Each step we take shapes our character and leads to our destiny.

The Beauty Way is the way of respectful balance. May your path lead you to your heart's true desire, and a life of abundant fulfillment, harmony, and bliss.

Walking in Beauty—A prayer from the Navajo Nation
<u>thebeautyway.net</u>

Today I will walk out, today everything unnecessary will leave me, I will be as I was before, I will have a cool breeze over my body. I will have a light body, I will be forever happy, nothing will hinder me.

> I walk with Beauty below me.
> I walk with Beauty above me.
> I walk with Beauty all around me.
> My words will be Beautiful.
> In Beauty, all day long, may I walk.
> Through the returning seasons, may I walk.
> On the trail marked with pollen, may I walk.
> With dew about my feet, may I walk.
> With Beauty before me, may I walk.
> With Beauty behind me, may I walk.
> With Beauty below me, may I walk.
> With Beauty above me, may I walk.
> With Beauty all around me, may I walk.
> In old age wandering a trail of Beauty,
> lively, may I walk.
> In old age wandering a trail of Beauty,
> living again, may I walk.
> It is finished in Beauty.
> It is finished in Beauty.
> Aho.

WRITING for SELF DETERMINATION

ASSIGNMENT VIII

Character offers a kind of freedom, and also requires responsibility. Questions to ask yourself about the state of your character include:

1. How do things that benefit you also benefit others?
2. How does your character influence others for better or worse? (consider how your character influences your family, friends, community, and beyond.)
3. How are you molding your character each and every day?
4. If character is our legacy—what will yours be?

...if that which you seek,
 you find not within yourself,
you will never find it without.
For behold,
I have been with you
from the beginning,
and I am that which is attained
at the end of desire."

~ Starhawk, Charge of the Goddess
 (adapted from Doreen Valiente version)

EXERCISE VIII

RECIPE FOR ABUNDANCE

Create a recipe for your life with the right balance of ingredience for you now.

Sample Recipe

Ingredients:

(cultivate the best quality ingredients possible)

- courage
- honor
- flexibility
- courtesy
- humility
- loyalty
- compassion
- fortitude
- sincerity
- humor
- harmony
- & integrity to hold ingredients together

Avoid salt. Salty = tough, aggressive
Avoid lemon. Bitter = sour, resentful
Add just a touch of sweetener.
Allow to ferment and grow!

APPENDIX A

12 TYPES OF STINKIN' THINKIN'

1. All-or-nothing thinking – this narrow thinking reduces options. When we see things as either/or and black/white, we are blind to the many real possibilities that exist in between.
2. Overgeneralization – this overly broad thinking is found in always/never statements.
3. Mental Filter – this selective thinking filters out the good stuff and focuses on the negative.
4. Discounting the positive – this distorted thinking minimizes the positive as irrelevant.
5. Jumping to conclusions – this overly quick thinking assumes the negative without evidence.
6. Mind Reading – this overly powerful thinking assumes the ability to read and interpret other's thoughts as negative.
7. Fortune-telling – this thinking is sometimes called *self fulfilling prophecy*: predicting a negative outcome before it happens.
8. Magnification – this distorted thinking exagerates the negative.
9. Emotional Reasoning – this thinking supports how we feel. Negative feelings are assumed to be accurate perceptions of reality. We assume that the negative emotion reflects the way things are.
10. "Should" statements – this judgmental thinking discounts the positive by focusing on what's missing.
11. Labeling – this rigid thinking keeps us stuck in negative absractions. Labels directed toward self or other, such as, "loser" "failure" or "jerk" petrify our perspective.
12. Personalization and Blame – this over-simplified thinking leads to guilt, shame, and feelings of inadequacy or anger by concentrating the negative on self or others.

Excerpted from Dr. David Burns, http://stinkin-thinkin.com/tag/david-d-burns/. See selected bibliography.

APPENDIX B

HOW TO WORD INTENTIONS

Make your wishes and hopes into intentions. Here are 12 sample intentions using positive, present, and specific language. These are examples based on emotional desires. Get creative and make up your own!

1. Peace is rooted in my soul and expands outward with each breath I take.
2. Wisdom guides my thoughts, decisions, and actions.
3. Compassion guides my thoughts, words, and deeds.
4. Joy blooms like a flower from me, and I spread it profusely wherever I go.
5. The flame of my inner fire is re-ignited, burning strong, giving me passionate energy.
6. Acceptance of myself and others lifts me from the pain of judgement.
7. Forgiveness, like a soothing salve, anoints my heart and soul.
8. Inner strength keeps me grounded today and everyday.
9. Inspiration moves me to creatively express myself unselfconsciously.
10. Nurtured by my self love, I overflow love onto others like a radiant sun-stream.
11. Happiness fills me to the brim.
12. Content, like a sleeping kitten, my mind relaxes.

APPENDIX C

HOW TO CHANT SOKA GAKKAI

Soka Gakkai is a Japanese Buddhist movement based on the teachings of the 13th-century Japanese priest Nichiren. It was founded by Daisaku Ikeda, Tsunesaburō Makiguchi, and Jōsei Toda in 1930.

To chant *Nam-myoho-renge-kyo* is to call forth your Buddha nature. Chant the mantra "Nam Myoho Renge Kyo," once in the morning and once at night. It translates to "Devotion to the Mystic Law of Cause and Effect through Sound", or "Glory to the Sutra of the Lotus of the Supreme Law." Or my own loose translation, "from the muck the flower grows."

Soka Gakkai International: https://www.sgi.org/

APPENDIX D

SHADOW WORK

Our shadow is made up of both dark and light. In addition to projecting our unwanted, negative traits, we also project our good traits onto others, disowning our potential. The shadow, for this reason, is called the seat of creativity—it holds the key to manifesting our desires. We are all creaters. Yet we may reject our creative ability: "Arts and crafts are great for others, but not for me." This is shadow talking. We each create each day of our lives.

5 STEPS TO LIGHTEN YOUR SHADOW

To lighten your shadow, become enlightened; shine a light on your shadow material by becoming more self aware:

1. Allow yourself to feel and acknowledge (but not act on) your emotions. Try to examine your feelings as if they were someone elses'.
2. When you see something you don't like in another, examine how you also manifest this trait.
3. When you are envious of another, examine how you also possess the trait you admire.
4. When you don't want to look at something, look deeper.

"All things are composed of Light in various frequencies that express as limitless forms. Some light frequencies are of greater density than others.

All shadows result from light hitting a dense object. Psychological shadows too. Therefore, it's good to become as translucent and translucid as possible to dispel lurking shadows.

If you must look at and/or deal with shadows, whether your own or another's, then refocus your Light on the object being illuminated, since that form is the source of the shadow.

Find the correct 4 angles of illuminating whatever you want to focus on, and all shadows will be dispelled. Then you're seeing things with an illuminated mind, and can act accordingly." From Robert Wilkinson, www.aquariuspapers.com.

SELECTED BIBLIOGRAPHY

Adler, Mortimer. *Six Great Ideas*. Simon & Schuster. 1981.

Am J. "Comparing the effects of physical practice and mental imagery rehearsal on learning basic surgical skills by medical students." Obstet. Gynecol. 2004 Nov;191(5):1811-4. https://www.ncbi.nlm.nih.gov/pubmed/15547570. Accessed 7/1/2018

Anson, Binh. Anson, Binh. BuddhaSasana. *The Five Hindrances*. Nivarana. Ajahn Brahmavamso. http://www.budsas.org/ebud/ebmed051.htm. Accessed 1/5/2018.

The Beauty Way blog. https://thebeautyway.net/. Accessed 1/5/2018.

Burns M.D., David D. *The Feeling Good Handbook*. William Morrow and Company. 1989.

Burroughs, Tony. *The Intenders of the Highest Good*. http://www.tonyburroughs.net/). Accessed 1/5/2018.

Byrne, Ronda. *The Secret*. Atria Books. 2006.

Cambridge Advanced Learner's Dictionary & Thesaurus© Cambridge University Press: Stinking Thinking. https://dictionary.cambridge.org/us/dictionary/english/stinking-thinking. Accessed 1/5/2018.

Carpenter, Harry W. The Genie Within: Your Subconcious Mind--How It Works and How to Use It. Harry Carpenter Publishing. 2003

Carroll, Lewis, *Through The Looking Glass*. 1871.

Castanada, Carlos. "Enemies of a man of knowledge." The Teachings of Don Juan: A Yaqui Way of Knowledge. 1998.

Collins Dictionary Online. https://www.collinsdictionary.com/us/dictionary/english/character-building. Accessed 1/5/2018.

The Compact Edition of the Oxford English Dictionary. Oxford Univ. Press. 1971.

Changemakers. https://www.changemakers.com/. Accessed 1/5/2018.

Diffen. Blog: diffen.com/difference/Ethics_vs_Morals. Accessed 1/5/2018.

Dijksterhuis, Ap. "Think Different: The Merits of Unconscious Thought in Preference Development and Decision Making." University of Amsterdam. Journal of Personality and Social Psychology, Vol. 87. 2004.

How to Create Abundance

Emmons & McCullough, "Gratitude and Well-Being" UC Berkley. 2003.

Ehrmann. Max. "Desiderata." *The Poems of Max Ehrmann.* 1948.
Hari, Johann. Chasing The Scream: The First And Last Days of the War on Drugs. /bloomsbury, NY.

Goldin, Dr. Phillipe. *The Neuroscience of Emotions*, Youtube video. https://www.youtube.com/watch?v=5wpHvbZCDa0. Accessed 1/5/2018.

Harris, A.H, Luskin, F.M., Benisovich, S.V., Standard, S., Bruning, J., Evans, S. and Thoresen, C. (2006) Effects of a group forgiveness intervention on forgiveness, perceived stress and trait anger: A randomized trial. Journal of Clinical Psychology. 62(6) 715-733.

Hauser, Marc. "Moral sense test." Harvard's Primate and Cognitive Neuroscience Laboratory. 2003.

Henepola Gunaratana, Bhante. "What Exactly is Vipassana Meditation?" Tricycle Magazine. https://tricycle.org/magazine/vipassana-meditation/. Accessed 1/5/2018.

Holland, H.S. "What is Character?" Art of Manliness, June 25, 2013. https://www.artofmanliness.com/2013/06/25/what-is-character-its-3-true-qualities-and-how-to-develop-it/. Accessed 1/5/2018.

Jacobs. Tom. "Study: Ethical People More Satisfied With Life." Pacific Standard Magazine. Nov 2, 2011; https://psmag.com/social-justice/study-ethical-people-more-satisfied-with-life-36792. Accessed 1/5/2018.

James, William. *The Principles of Psychology.* 1890.

Kassar, Tim. *The High Price of Materialism, A Bradford Book, 2003.*

Keirstead, Cheri Christine. "Ancient Practice Of Forgiveness – Ho'oponopono." *Live In Harmony With Your Soul.* Http://Cherivalentine.Com/Hooponopono/. Accessed 1/5/2018.

Lyubomirsky, Sonja. *The How of Happiness A Scientific Approach to getting the life you want, The Penguin Press, NY 2008.*

Maddi, Salvatore, founder of the Hardiness Institute, "The HardiSurvey®." http://www.hardinessinstitute.com/?page_id=1195. Accessed 1/5/2018.

Mahlum, Anne. *Back on My Feet.* https://www.annemahlum.com/bomf. Accessed 1/5/2018.

Bibliography

Manson, Mark. On Happiness. http://markmanson.net/. Accessed 1/5/2018.

Marsdon, Jim. "A Journey of Transformation." On Being Magazine, June 25, 2016, https://onbeing.org/blog/the-journey-of-transformation/. Accessed 1/5/2018.

McGill, Bryant. Voice of Reason: Speaking to the Great and Good Spirit of Revolution of Mind. The Paperlyon Publishing Company, Fl. 2012.

Meadows, Kenneth. *Earth Medicine: Revealing Hidden Teachings of the Native American Medicine Wheel*. Earth Quest. May 1, 1996.

Merriam Webster Online Dictionary. https://www.merriam-webster.com/dictionary/energy. Accessed 1/5/2018.

Mesher, Alan. *The Silent Steps of Grace, A Gripping Tale of Tragedy, Transformation, and Triumph*. Kindle. 2012.

Miller, Ruth PhD. "What's the difference between feelings, thoughts, and emotions?" Original publication date May 2011. http://revruthlmiller.com/2011/05/. Accessed 1/5/2018.

Musser, George. "Quantum Links In Time And Space May Form The Universe's Foundation," Science Magazine, 1/23/2016, https://www.wired.com/2016/01/quantum-links-in-time-and-space-may-form-the-universes-foundation/. Accessed 1/5/2018.

Newberg M.D., Andrew, Waldman, Mark Robert. "The Most Dangerous Word in the World" Psychology Today. August, 2012. https://www.psychologytoday.com/blog/words-can-change-your-brain/201208/the-most-dangerous-word-in-the-world. Accessed 1/5/2018.

Oxford Online Dictionary. https://en.oxforddictionaries.com/definition/hygge. Accessed 1/5/2018.

Oxford Online Dictionary. https://en.oxforddictionaries.com/definition/virtue. Accessed 1/5/2018.

Penrose, Roger. The Emperor's New Mind: Concerning Computers, Minds and The Laws of Physics. Oxford University Press. 1989.

Plotkin, Bill. "Nature and the Human Soul." http://www.natureandthehumansoul.com/newbook/introduction.htm. Accessed 1/5/2018.

Post, Stephen & Neimark, Jill . *Why Good Things Happen to Good People: How to Live a Longer, Healthier, Happier Life by the Simple Act of Giving*, Broadway Books, 2007.

How to Create Abundance

Robertson, Ian H. The *Winner Effect: The Neuroscience of Success and Failure*. Thomas Dunne Books. 2013.

Sams, Jamie. *Earth Medicine*. Harper Collins. 1994.

Schröder, Tobias; Stewart, Terrence C.; Paul Thagard. "Intention, Emotion, and Action: A Neural Theory Based on Semantic Pointers."

Science Daily, "People show more humorous creativity when primed with thoughts of death." https://www.sciencedaily.com/releases/2013/07/130702100339.htm. Accessed 1/5/2018.

"The Secrets Of The World's Luckiest People." Huffington Post Healthy Living. 11/14/2013. https://www.huffingtonpost.com/2013/11/14/is-luck-a-skill_n_4225951.html. Accessed 1/5/2018.

Simmons, Daniel. *The Monkey Business*. Video uploaded April 2016. https://www.youtube.com/watch?v=ux1cL7tHjlI. Accessed 1/5/2018.

Span, Paula. "Are Caregivers Healthier?" The New York Times, October 1, 2013. https://newoldage.blogs.nytimes.com/2013/10/31/are-caregivers-healthier/. Accessed 1/5/2018.

Susman, Warren. Culture as History. Penguin Random House; ebook publication. 2012.

Valiente, Doreen. adapted by Starhawk. "Charge of the Goddess." *The Spiral Dance*. 1979.

Sutriasa, Shakti. "3 Reasons Why Taking Responsibility Is Spiritual." *Huffington Post 2-4-2017*, https://www.huffingtonpost.com/shakti-sutriasa-lcsw-ma/3-reasons-why-taking-resp_b_9150188.html. Accessed 1/5/2018.

Swiftdeer Reagan, Harley. Dear Tribe Metis-Medicine Society. http://deer-tribe.com/. Accessed 1/5/2018.

The Daily Stoic. https://dailystoic.com/what-is-stoicism-a-definition-3-stoic-exercises-to-get-you-started/. Accessed 1/5/2018.

Two Feathers, Kainaiwa Clan of the Blackfoot. Native American's Online http://www.native-americans-online.com/native-american-warrior.html. Accessed 1/5/2018.

Urban Dictionary Online. https://www.urbandictionary.com/define.php?term=in+the+zone. Accessed 1/5/2018.

Bibliography

Waldman, Mark. "10 Mind Blowing Discoveries About the Human Brain." *NeuroWisdom and the Secrets to Happiness and Success*. 2014. http://van-burenpublishing.com/wp-content/uploads/1-NeuroWisdom-Ebook1.pdf. Accessed 1/5/2018.

Webster online dictionary. https://www.merriam-webster.com/dictionary/hardiness?utm_campaign=sd&utm_medium=serp&utm_source=jsonld. Accessed 1/5/2018.

"What Is Stoicism? A Definition & 3 Stoic Exercises To Get You Started." https://stoic-leaders.com/what-stoicism-definition-stoic-exercises/. Accessed 1/5/2018.

Whitman, Walt. "Song of the Open Road." *Leaves of Grass*. 1856.

Wiley Online Library, Cognative Science a Multidisciplinary Journal, Nov 2013.

Wilkinson, Robert. Author and publisher, "www.aquariuspapers.com." Accessed 1/5/2018.

ABOUT THE AUTHOR

Mitch Cearbhall is a teacher, student, and researcher on topics from conflict management to spiritual and personal development, focusing on consciousness studies and new interpretations of quantum mechanics. He is an advocate of non-violent communication.

Contact Mitch at: https://anamcara-press.com/contact-us/

www.ingramcontent.com/pod-product-compliance
Lightning Source LLC
Chambersburg PA
CBHW021442080526
44588CB00009B/651